Measuring Software Design Quality

David N. Card
Computer Sciences Corporation

with

Robert L. Glass
Computing Trends

Prentice Hall, Englewood Cliffs, New Jersey 07632

Library of Congress Cataloging-in-Publication Data

Card, David N.
    Measuring software design quality / David N. Card with Robert L.
Glass.
        p.   cm.
    Bibliography: p.
    Includes index.
    ISBN 0-13-568593-1
    1. Computer software--Quality control.   I. Glass, Robert L.,
1932-   . II. Title.
QA76.76.Q35C37 1990
005.1--dc20   89-15939
                                                         CIP

Editorial/production supervision and
interior design: **Brendan M. Stewart**
Manufacturing buyer: **Robert Anderson**

This book can be made available to businesses
and organizations at a special discount when
ordered in large quantities. For more information
contact:

Prentice-Hall, Inc.
Special Sales and Markets
College Division
Englewood Cliffs, N.J. 07632

 © 1990 by Prentice-Hall, Inc.
A Division of Simon & Schuster
Englewood Cliffs, New Jersey 07632

Printed in the United States of America
10 9 8 7 6 5 4 3 2 1

ISBN 0-13-568593-1

Prentice-Hall International (UK) Limited, *London*
Prentice-Hall of Australia Pty. Limited, *Sydney*
Prentice-Hall Canada Inc., *Toronto*
Prentice-Hall Hispanoamericana, S.A., *Mexico*
Prentice-Hall of India Private Limited, *New Delhi*
Prentice-Hall of Japan, Inc., *Tokyo*
Simon & Schuster Asia Pte. Ltd., *Singapore*
Editora Prentice-Hall do Brasil, Ltda., *Rio de Janeiro*

This book is dedicated to all those software practitioners who care about doing a good job, succeed in spite of the obstacles, and still look for better ways of doing things.

Contents

Foreword

Dave Card lights up a cloudy metrics landscape with *Measuring Software Design Quality*. He brings fresh ideas to a critical research area and, equally important, he shows us how to use these design metrics in our software projects.

The value of this book is directly traceable to:

- the pivotal role of software design in the performance, reliability, and safety of complex systems;
- the persistent high cost of software development;
- the acute need for effective measures of software process and product characteristics.

Most of the software measures now used in organizations and featured in measurement tools emerged from a flurry of activity in the mid- to late 1970s. In some areas, like complexity, the popular metrics are unchanged over the past ten years. The slow pace of metrics research was shown in a survey conducted in the Software Engineering Laboratory at NASA's Goddard Space Flight Center. Participants in the Tenth Annual Software Engineering Workshop singled out software metrics as an area in which progress has been very disappointing. After a decade of so few advances, this book is especially welcome.

Dave Card has set upon a challenging course. The title alone—*Measuring Software Design Quality*—is daring. What title could lay out a more difficult assignment? As measurement goes, this is tough stuff. We in software have often taken our cues from more established disciplines. Measurement of physical reality, we learned, involved three elements: an object, an observable characteristic, and an apparatus for performing the measurement. The measurement examples, giving instances of object/observable/apparatus—"table/length/yardstick,"—were clear enough. Well, it's a long, long way from "table/length/yardstick" to "software/ design quality/design quality analyzer." In each of the three elements of measurement, we have major problems. Our "object," software, is invisible and intangible. Our "observable," design quality, raises the issue: What is quality? What is the relative importance of simplicity, maintainability, efficiency, and other characteristics that contribute to design quality? Our "apparatus" is often a tool that processes the source code for what it reveals of design because earlier design descriptions are seldom complete or formally represented.

Measurement of some key software characteristics—like complexity and quality—has less in common with "table/length/yardstick" and more similarity to measurement in quantum mechanics. These software characteristics are "latent" observables that lie quietly beneath the surface until we—in roles as reviewer or maintainer—or other systems interact with the software. The measured value then depends in an essential way on the circumstances of the operations performed during the interaction.

Dave Card knows the operations performed on software. The strength of his book is his recognition and understanding of measures as more than numbers but rather as reflecting a model of the process of software design and development. We in turn have confidence in the measures because they relate to activities and decisions that we see in our design work. Dave brings together micro- and macro-level design metrics as a natural consequence of considering the varying granularity used in thinking about design.

Don't be misled by the simplicity of the metrics in this book. Examples abound in science and engineering of simple relationships whose consequences are not. In software design, simplicity is a virtue; and in software design metrics, it is no less valuable. With simple metrics, the required data collection is less costly, the prospects for effective use are heightened, and the correspondence of the metrics to process activities is easier to establish.

This book is a concrete instance of that elusive buzzword "technology transfer." By contributing his extensive practical experience and communication skills, Bob Glass has helped Dave to produce a book that presents recent research results in a way that they can be used by practitioners in design reviews, project planning, quality assurance, and similar tasks.

This book will stimulate the reader's thinking about ways to improve the measurement and management of software development: measuring software design quality is a difficult task; *Measuring Software Design Quality* is a strong contribution.

William W. Agresti
Silver Spring, Maryland

Preface

Currently, measurement plays only a small role in software development practice, mostly confined to cost estimation. This book describes other roles for software measurement in design engineering, quality control, and technology evaluation. Most measurement books take an encyclopedic approach in which every thing possible is measured. That tends to make measurement an onerous burden to software developers.

Instead, this book proposes a small set of measures centered around design quality. The consequences of design quality (or lack thereof) propagate throughout the software life cycle. This approach to measurement provides a new perspective for viewing software development and design, in particular. It leads to a better understanding of what a good design is and challenges some widely accepted design practices. Rather than propose a new design methodology, we describe how measurement works with a specific set of methods to ensure a good design. Measures are meaningless until related to a method. Without measures, methods are not engineering.

This book provides the practitioner with criteria for improving software designs to promote productivity, quality, and maintainability. It is intended for use as a reference by software development managers, lead software engineers, and software product assurance personnel. Other researchers may want to compare methods and results. Although my experience with structured design and FORTRAN programming leads me to use examples and data from those areas, these measurement concepts can be generalized to most design methods and languages.

This book integrates the results of several years of software engineering research as well as practical experience in software quality assurance. Although I performed substantial original research leading to this manuscript, its foundation was laid by the efforts of others. Because one of my goals is to highlight the underlying harmony of diverse software measurement results, I have cited these results extensively in the text. The reader will find many thoughtful and stimulating articles among the references. In particular, my approach (although substantially less ambitious) was inspired by Tom DeMarco's *Controlling Software Projects*.

The book's chapters and appendixes are organized into four parts. Part 1 provides background material. Chapter 1 presents a general discussion of the nature of software, its quality, design, and measurement. It is argued that the related attributes of complexity, modularity, and produceability are the key discriminators of a good software design. Chapter 2 describes two examples of data collection programs and defines a minimum measurement set.

Part 2 describes the evolution of the design complexity model proposed in this book as the basis for software product engineering. Chapter 3 reviews two milestones in the development of software complexity measures (software science and cyclomatic number). Chapter 4 discusses the results of efforts to measure the particular aspect of design quality known as modularity.

Chapter 5 explains the comprehensive software complexity model derived from this experience. It shows how complexity differs from functional allocation to system design to unit design. It provides guidelines for engineering design to optimize software cost and size, error rate, and maintainability. It demonstrates the validity of the complexity model using data from actual projects.

Part 3 identifies the other principal uses of measures. It explains how measures can be applied by managers during software development to support cost estimation (Chap. 6), quality control (Chap. 7), and process improvement (Chap. 8). Finally, Chap. 9 reiterates the book's central ideas about software design engineering, quality, and measurement. Part 4 provides additional details and supporting materials for topics introduced elsewhere in the book.

Aside from the appendixes (Part 4), this short book is best read in its entirety.

David N. Card

In the broad world of computer science and software engineering, there is a small but significant number of beacons of light. At each of those beacons, some person or collection of persons is doing some original and significant work that illuminates the world for the rest of us. Dave Card is one of those beacons of light. With access to the real world of the practitioner, and with deep understanding and caring about the world of theory and research, Dave creates an all too rare blend of *practical theory,* the kind of theory that can be shown to have a basis in reality.

It is especially rewarding to me to identify and work with a beacon of light in industry. Although the bounds of brilliance are not the ivy-covered walls around academic institutions, too often the brilliance of the industry practitioner is focused inward only on corporate goals rather than outward on the literature and the profession. Dave Card is an exception to that rule.

When I first encountered this manuscript, Dave was struggling to find the time and energy to put the finishing touches on what was obviously an important book-to-be. Because of the value in what I saw Dave preparing to present here, I offered to help him with that time and energy problem. The result is our first collaboration. I hope it will not be the last.

It is well known that industry software practitioners are infrequent buyers of books. That means that the books they *do* choose must be important and definitive, not "yet another book about structured poobah." I believe that here Dave Card has one of those important and definitive books. I commend it to my practitioner colleagues. And, of course, anything that important to a practitioner should be must reading to the academician as well.

Robert L. Glass
Pittsburgh, PA

Acknowledgments

The initial research phase of this project benefited from the substantial support of Frank E. McGarry, Dr. Victor R. Basili, Dr. Gerald T. Page, and other personnel involved in the NASA/GSFC Software Engineering Laboratory. In particular, I want to recognize the valuable insights offered by Dr. William W. Agresti and Victor E. Church during the drafting of the manuscript. They also played important roles in part of the research described here. Robert L. Glass helped me frame the original manuscript to attract a wider audience. Together with Dr. Richard H. Thayer, he also provided me with the moral support and encouragement to publish this material.

I also want to thank Dr. Arturo Silvestrini, as representative for all my unnamed colleagues at Computer Sciences Corporation who contributed to this work through discussions and by practical example. Lynn Bosmajian and his team deserve special mention for their excellent work in preparing the graphics. Barbara Segrist provided valuable editorial assistance throughout the project.

David N. Card

1

Making Software Design an Engineering Discipline

The importance of design to software engineering is increasing. Although traditional rules of thumb estimate the proportion of development effort spent in design at 40 percent, recent estimates show an increase to about 60 percent for new methods. Thus, getting a good design is ever more essential to successful software development. This book describes an approach to measuring software design quality. By supplying an element missing from most design methods—measurement—we begin to move software design from an art toward an engineering discipline.

In what follows, we will focus on the two basic questions faced by all software measurement practitioners:

Q: What data (measurements) should be collected?
A: The approximately 20 items listed in Fig. 2–3 are the minimum.
Q: What should be done with the data once collected?
A: Product design engineering (Part II) and project management (Part III).

Of course, these questions are interrelated; answering one constrains the other: Available data limit possible uses, and intended uses define necessary data. This book represents a sort of convergence after many iterations of questions and answers. However, no single formula will satisfy all variations of a complex process like software development. Every organization needs to develop its own measurement program. Here, we describe one approach to doing that.

Rather than setting out to measure everything at once, our approach focuses initially on software design quality and then extends to encompass other areas of software development in less detail. Because design is a broad and important topic in software engineering, it provides a good starting point for any software measurement program. However, before discussing details, let's review some basic issues regarding software measurement, design, and quality. Although this book is not primarily about quality assurance or software engineering methods, many references to those topics will be necessary.

1-1 MEASUREMENT ISSUES

The infrastructure supporting software practitioners has grown dramatically over the past few years. In particular, many new methods and tools intended to enhance software design have been developed and come into widespread use. Corresponding advances in measurement are needed: to help software engineers make design decisions and to provide managers with visibility into the software process and product.

Industry, in general, recognizes three historical levels of quality assurance technology [83]:

1. *Product inspection* (c. 1920)—examining intermediate and final products to detect defects
2. *Process control* (c. 1960)—monitoring defect rates to identify defective process elements and control the process
3. *Design improvement* (c. 1980)—engineering the design of the process and the product to minimize the potential for defects

Currently, most software enterprises rest comfortably at level 1, relying on a system of inspections and reviews to ensure quality. Achievement of levels 2 and 3 depends on increasingly sophisticated forms of measurement. For example, improving the design of a software product requires accurate predictions of its performance during later development and operation.

To date, the only generally accepted use for any software measures is in cost estimation. For example, a 1983 survey [1] of software quality assurance practice showed that 42 percent of organizations used conformance to standards, 38 percent relied on professional judgment, and only 12 percent used numerical methods to judge software quality. Why is this true in software engineering when, at the same time, everyone seems to accept the axiom that measurement is the basis of science and engineering?

Part of the difficulty is inherent in the nature of software development. It is an intellectual nondeterministic process. Moreover, software specification, design, and implementation are closely intertwined. In particular, software design has been described as a "wicked problem." That is, the problem cannot be definitively stated, nor can it be determined when the problem has been completely solved. Thus, measurement must be difficult.

Still, much of the fault lies in the nature of the design measures proposed. Most of the early measures were derived from source code. Who is going to rewrite a working program to improve its score on a "theoretical" quality measure—especially when the measures can only be computed by an expensive source analyzer package after the job is done? The greatest potential leverage for software measurement lies in design, not code, analysis.

Kearney et al. [2] point to several other reasons why software complexity measures in particular have failed thus far. Most measures are proposed without a clearly formulated theory or model of the activity being measured. Many measures have no obvious practical application. Few measures have been empirically validated. Kearney et al. [2] warn that the use of poorly constructed and misunderstood measures can actually degrade software development performance by rewarding poor practice. Browne and Shaw [3] voiced similar concerns even earlier.

Because many of these problems result from inadequate definition of methods and goals, this exposition will go to considerable lengths to set the stage for the empirical results of Parts II and III of this book. The general measurement approach followed includes five steps:

1. Define the object of measurement (i.e., software design). Often this means developing a model of the object.
2. Identify the characteristics or attributes to be measured (i.e., quality).
3. Specify the purpose or intended use of the measurement results.
4. Collect data as indicated by steps 1, 2, and 3.
5. Verify and/or modify the model based on analysis and application experience with the collected data.

Although each of these steps will be discussed in turn, most of the emphasis in succeeding chapters (especially in Parts II and III) will be on the empirical results of step 5.

The approach described in this book attempts to avoid those pitfalls already mapped by measurement pioneers. It traces another step toward an overall metrics-guided methodology for software development (see Ramamoorthy et al. [4] for a requirements analysis example). Measures cannot replace good methods, but they can help to ensure good design products and an efficient development process. Without measurement, software methods are not engineering.

1-2 SOFTWARE DESIGN

Measurement begins with a theory or model of the object to be measured. Many different definitions of and methods for software design have been advanced. All have their adherents and detractors. This book will explain a very simple model of software design (some may say simplistic) that leads to simple but useful measures. In some sense, this model represents the least common denominator among the various design approaches. The model derives from a particular view of the software development process in which design occurs.

This conceptual model actually functions in a real world where budgets and schedules are major concerns. Usually, it is embedded in a software life cycle (like Fig. 1-1). To some extent, the life cycle notion of discrete software development phases is a response to the lack of more detailed software development measures. ''Completing'' a phase gives the manager a general sense of well-being and progress but not much specific information on the quantity or quality of work performed. High-level reviews usually encompass whatever has been done to date, rather than marking completion of predefined units of work.

Figure 1-2 highlights the design part of a conventional software development life cycle (the one used throughout this book). Software design involves three activities: functional allocation, system design, and unit design. Each activity employs different methods and achieves different objectives. This book will show that the nature of software quality also differs from one activity to another. Note that these software design activities occur in three chronological phases: preliminary design, detailed design, and unit design. However, the three activities do not map onto the phases in a one-to-one relationship. Each phase involves multiple activities.

During functional allocation (most of preliminary design), the designers collect related requirements into functional groups and identify dependencies among functions. External interfaces must also be defined. Figure 1-3 shows the subsystems and data sets of an example system. The detailed results of functional allocation may be represented as a data flow diagram, high-level structure chart, or as a simple list of requirements by subsystems. The preliminary design review assesses the quality of the functional allocation.

During system design, the overall architecture of the system is defined, primarily through partitioning. Functional decomposition, information hiding, and data

DESIGN		IMPLEMENTATION			TEST	
PRELIMINARY DESIGN	DETAILED DESIGN	UNIT DESIGN	UNIT CODE	UNIT TEST	INTEGRATION TEST	SYSTEM TEST

Figure 1-1.   Software life cycle definition

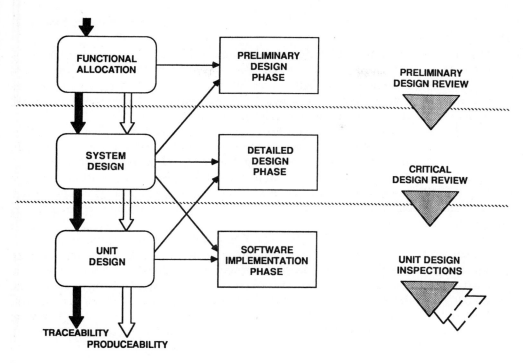

Figure 1–2. Views of software design

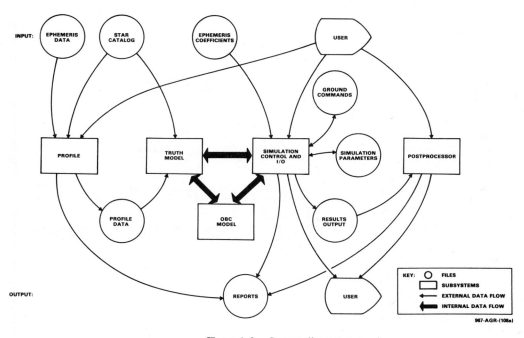

Figure 1–3. System diagram example

abstraction are examples of architectural design strategies. This step in design allocates data and functions to individual units or design parts. The structure chart (see Fig. 1–4) is commonly used to represent the architectural design for functional decomposition. Internal interfaces must be defined during this step too. The critical design review assesses the quality of system design.

During unit design, the structure of each component of the system architecture is elaborated. Typically, this means defining algorithms and data structures that convert the input into the required final output or some other intermediate form. At this step, a lot of application- and implementation-specific information (not contained in the requirements) must be added to the design. Unit design is most often represented as prologs and pseudocode (see Fig. 1–5). Each unit undergoes a design inspection at completion.

Design primarily encompasses partitioning and elaboration activities. Through the early stages of design, many details remain unspecified. Each later step involves some ''rediscovery'' of earlier design information and decisions. Understanding a particular part of a design requires looking at its context (e.g., other connected parts). Thus, the magnitude and nature of those connections affect the ease of proceeding to the next step. Ideally, at the end of design activities, the system has been fully defined in some formal or semiformal notation ready for coding.

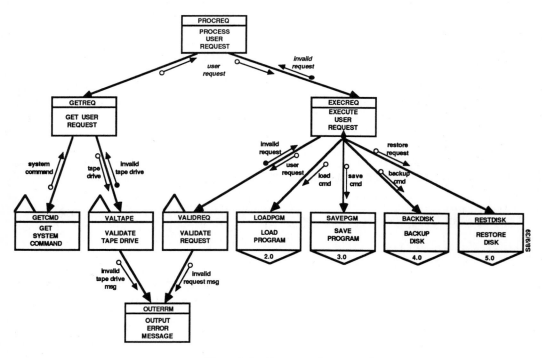

Figure 1–4.   Structure chart example

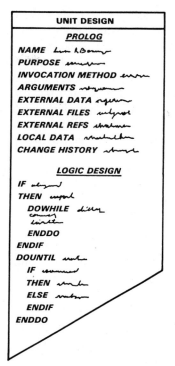

Figure 1-5. Unit design example

Design serves as a template for assembling code. Little understanding by the programmer leads to difficulty in implementing and maintaining the software. One part of understandability relates to presentation, including conformance to standards of good practice and consistent use of a common notation. Another part is complexity, the number and nature of items and their relationships in the design. Because coding is largely a translation process (once design is complete), most software complexity resides in the design.

The partitioning accomplished during system design allows individual units to be assigned to different programmers so that implementation can proceed in parallel. As unit design progresses, changes in the system design may be required in response to both internal and external stimuli: Requirements change; design parts can't be fully independent; the design must preserve traceability to requirements. Thus, design activities continue throughout software development.

Because the design processes of partitioning and elaboration are largely intellectual, it is difficult to measure them directly. Fortunately, the effects of these processes (e.g., complexity and modularity) can readily be observed in design products (e.g., structure charts, prologs, and pseudocode). Although most researchers (including these authors) have focused on analyzing the design product, some promising studies of the process itself have begun.

1-3 SOFTWARE QUALITY

The next step in measurement is to define characteristics or attributes of the object to be measured. The term *software quality* has been interpreted in many different ways. McCall [5] provides the definition of software quality most widely used within the software engineering world. Table 1-1 lists a set of software-specific quality factors. McCall breaks each of these factors down into criteria, each of which has specific metrics associated with it. These metrics include both subjective judgments and objective measures. The complete structure involves several hundred data items. However, these quality factors capture characteristics of the final product rather than its design (the focus of this discussion). The list (Table 1-1) consists of general requirements that a specific customer may or may not want to emphasize in a given software product.

Basili [6] proposes a three-step approach to selecting measures in general, not just quality measures: (1) Identify organizational goals, (2) define questions relevant to the goals, and (3) select measures that answer the questions. Data collection follows from this. This approach results in a measurement suite customized to organizational information needs and capabilities. Thus, quality takes on a special local

TABLE 1-1.   DEFINITION OF SOFTWARE QUALITY FACTORS

FACTOR	DEFINITION
CORRECTNESS	EXTENT TO WHICH A PROGRAM SATISFIES ITS SPECIFICATIONS AND FULFILLS THE USER'S MISSION OBJECTIVES
RELIABILITY	EXTENT TO WHICH A PROGRAM CAN BE EXPECTED TO PERFORM ITS INTENDED FUNCTION WITH REQUIRED PRECISION
EFFICIENCY	AMOUNT OF COMPUTING RESOURCES AND CODE REQUIRED BY A PROGRAM TO PERFORM A FUNCTION
INTEGRITY	EXTENT TO WHICH ACCESS TO SOFTWARE OR DATA BY UNAUTHORIZED PERSONS CAN BE CONTROLLED
USABILITY	EFFORT REQUIRED TO LEARN, OPERATE, PREPARE INPUT, AND INTERPRET OUTPUT OF A PROGRAM
MAINTAINABILITY	EFFORT REQUIRED TO LOCATE AND FIX AN ERROR IN AN OPERATIONAL PROGRAM
TESTABILITY	EFFORT REQUIRED TO TEST A PROGRAM TO ENSURE THAT IT PERFORMS ITS INTENDED FUNCTION
FLEXIBILITY	EFFORT REQUIRED TO MODIFY AN OPERATIONAL PROGRAM
PORTABILITY	EFFORT REQUIRED TO TRANSFER A PROGRAM FROM ONE HARDWARE CONFIGURATION AND/OR SOFTWARE SYSTEM ENVIRONMENT TO ANOTHER
REUSABILITY	EXTENT TO WHICH A PROGRAM CAN BE USED IN OTHER APPLICATIONS; RELATED TO THE PACKAGING AND SCOPE OF THE FUNCTIONS THAT PROGRAMS PERFORM
INTEROPERABILITY	EFFORT REQUIRED TO COUPLE ONE SYSTEM WITH ANOTHER

ADAPTED FROM J. A. McCALL, P. K. RICHARDS, AND G. F. WALTERS, <u>FACTORS IN SOFTWARE QUALITY</u>, TABLE 3.1-1, ROME AIR DEVELOPMENT CENTER, RADC-TR-77-369, NOVEMBER 1977

meaning. The goal of this book is to establish some common criteria for software design quality and procedures for software measurement upon which organizations can expand by applying methods like Basili's [6].

Another view of software quality includes its relationship to reliability and safety. Figure 1–6 shows that quality is necessary (but not sufficient) to achieve high reliability and safety. Generally, problems begin with a conceptual (design) error by a software developer. (Of course, transcription and other errors occur too.) That error may be implemented in the software as one or more faults (sections of source code or documents that must be changed to fix the error). Often faults are detected only when they manifest themselves as failures (instances when the system performs in some manner other than that intended). A serious failure or combination of failures may result in an accident. Fault rate is a major factor in software reliability and safety and thus in software quality. This view shows the importance of software quality but only defines it in terms of its absence—here, the presence of faults.

Many software organizations approach quality in terms of conformance to standards—the degree to which the software satisfies prescribed criteria for format and content. Glass [7] argues that most software shops have too many standards and too little enforcement—that is, standards are too voluminous to be enforced. Often determination of conformance is subjective. For example, the directive to ''use meaningful variable names'' requires costly human verification. Although generating lots of standards may ease the manager's conscience, it does not ensure software quality.

Quality as Fitness for Use

This book adopts an industrial viewpoint on software quality. Juran, the noted industrial quality expert, defines product quality as ''fitness for use'' [8]. This concept

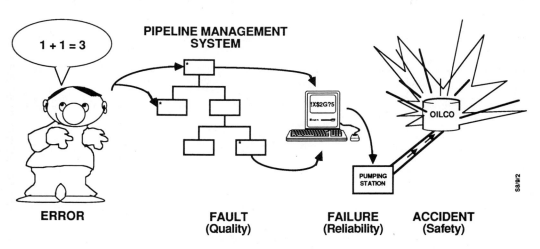

Figure 1–6. Types of software problems

includes all those features of the product recognized as beneficial to the user(s). Therefore, any attribute of the product that interferes with an intended use becomes a symptom of poor quality. However, as Fig. 1-7 shows, software development produces a series of products (with some intermediate users); each of these products involves fitness for use considerations.

For example, looking at design quality as fitness for use yields two principal uses of design for which its fitness must be assessed. First, the software design defines the functionality and performance of the final product for the operational user. Second, the software design provides a template for the production of the operational product by programmers and maintainers (intermediate users). If a design achieves both of these goals, we say it represents a "feasible" solution.

Thus, the essential components of software design fitness for use include

1. *Service in operation*—the degree to which the designed system meets the specified needs of the operational user. These may include both functional and performance requirements. From the software design point of view, "service in operation" equates to "satisfaction of requirements." This means showing traceability from requirements to design.

2. *Ease of production*—the ease and accuracy with which the design can be implemented and the product maintained. This includes aspects of technical ex-

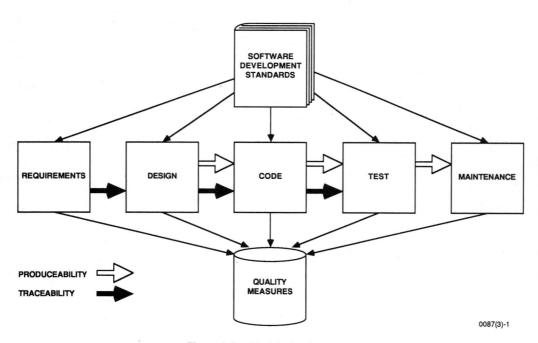

Figure 1-7.   Model of software quality

cellence like modularity and simplicity. Poor produceability (or manufacturability) means a high error rate, low productivity, and difficult maintenance.

Following appropriate software standards or guidelines may promote fitness for use in general ways, but it does not guarantee the traceability or produceability of a given software design. Standards address only a few aspects of software quality. Moreover, the inflexible application of standards often obscures the technical quality issues that they were developed to address. As Fig. 1-7 indicates, standards are "input" to the process, not performance-sensitive "output" from it. This book offers, instead, a flexible measurement-based approach to ensuring software quality that complements standards-based approaches.

Software Produceability

Because the nature of software quality differs from that of most other manufactured products with respect to cost, reliability, and maintainability, produceability is a very different consideration in software development from its role in manufacturing. Most of the cost of producing software comes from the design, implementation, and maintenance of the first (and often only) copy. For other products, development costs can be recaptured by selling multiple copies. For large software systems, getting the first copy right makes or breaks the product (and sometimes the producer as well).

Ideally, manufactured products are delivered fault-free (or rejected). Reliability, then, concerns the failure rate of components during use. Software doesn't wear out but may be delivered and put into operation with undiscovered flaws. The discovery of flaws during operation results in failures. Software maintenance involves adding new capabilities and fixing newly discovered errors rather than plugging in replacement parts. These factors are what make produceability in software development so different from manufacturing.

Figure 1-8 illustrates the importance of design produceability to software quality. The figure shows the distribution of errors by source from three actual software development projects studied by Weiss and Basili [9]. Values shown are medians. Figure 1-8 indicates that the bulk of nontranscription errors (detected during testing) relate in some way to software design, although at very detailed levels in many cases. Other published figures show design errors ranging from 55 to 85 percent of all software errors. The most popular estimate is probably 65 percent. Clearly, getting a good design is essential to software success.

Figures of Merit

Although Chap. 7 briefly discusses satisfaction of requirements and conformance to standards, most of this book deals with the more nebulous issue of produceability. In this sense, poor design quality results in high error rates, low productivity,

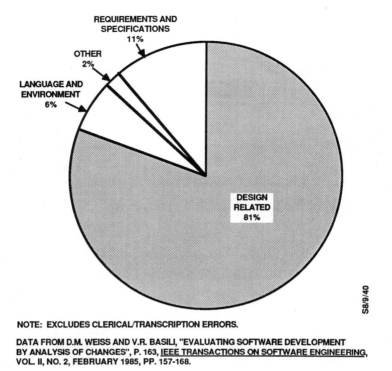

NOTE: EXCLUDES CLERICAL/TRANSCRIPTION ERRORS.

DATA FROM D.M. WEISS AND V.R. BASILI, "EVALUATING SOFTWARE DEVELOPMENT BY ANALYSIS OF CHANGES", P. 163, IEEE TRANSACTIONS ON SOFTWARE ENGINEERING, VOL. II, NO. 2, FEBRUARY 1985, PP. 157-168.

Figure 1-8. Sources of software errors

and poor maintainability. While most projects will have other fitness for use considerations too (portability, user-friendliness, etc.), concern for these three factors is common to most, if not all, software development projects. As in manufacturing enterprises, the software engineer optimizes design in terms of produceability to facilitate delivery of a good product. (See [80] for a discussion of product design guidelines for maximizing manufacturability.)

This book proposes "figures of merit" for software design quality to be used by engineers and managers. A figure of merit only indicates quality; it does not determine it. For example, poor design produceability suggests that errors and rework should be expected during implementation. However, an unusually skillful programming team might manage to avoid those problems. In the case of software design, understanding modularity and controlling complexity are the keys to managing produceability. Chapter 5 defines some figures of merit based on a quantitative model of software design and shows how they can be used to optimize design in terms of produceability.

1-4 MEASUREMENT APPLICATIONS

A successful measurement program establishes well-defined uses for measures. Both engineers and managers can benefit from measurement. Measures help to design a quality product and control the production process. Poor management leads to project failure at least as often as poor technical approach. During design and implementation, the project manager needs to predict, monitor, and control cost and quality performance.

Software design is the product engineering part of software development. Programming is in some ways analogous to the manufacturing part. Thus, design specifies the software solution that will eventually be implemented in the "concrete" of code. Before pouring concrete into that mold (the product design), we must assure ourselves that it has the right shape and sufficient strength for our needs. Most software design methods handle the quality issue by asserting that if the designer follows some prescribed rules, good design cannot be avoided. Yet there are plenty of examples of poor products being produced with good methods. That's what makes it hard to identify the good methods.

Moreover, software design is not a deterministic process. Two designers working from the same specification with the same methods may well produce different good designs, both of which satisfy requirements and conform to standards. In other engineering disciplines, design proceeds iteratively: An initial design is proposed, then measurement-based calculations assess its "quality," a prototype may be developed, then redesign occurs. Texts on software design recommend developing several alternative designs and choosing the best. In this case, can the "best" design be identified? Do any quantitative criteria exist?

These considerations suggest four basic uses of software measures:

1. *Project estimation*—predicting costs and developing schedules for future projects based on past performance
2. *Quality control*—assessing quality performance and determining the need for corrective action
3. *Process analysis*—identifying bottlenecks and leverage points in the software process, as well as evaluating new technology
4. *Product engineering*—making engineering decisions and choosing among product design alternatives

The first two applications, estimation and control, correspond to level 2 quality assurance technology (see Sec. 1-1). The last two applications, process analysis and product engineering, correspond to level 3. Every software enterprise should perform these functions and needs a measurement program to help achieve success.

1-5 ORGANIZATION OF THE BOOK

Chapter 2 explains some measurement principles and describes the example measurement programs from which the results discussed elsewhere were obtained. The rest of this book discusses quantitative strategies for measuring design quality and managing software development. An extensive base of empirical evidence supports the recommendations for data collection and measurement application made here.

Part II describes the design engineering applications of software measures. Within Part II, Chap. 3 reviews some early concepts of complexity; Chap. 4 examines the notion of modularity and its relationship to produceability; and Chap. 5 defines some figures of merit based on a quantitative model of software design and shows how they can be used to optimize design in terms of produceability.

Part III shows how managers use software measures to estimate costs (Chap. 6) and control quality (Chap. 7) and to evaluate technology (Chap. 8). Chapter 9 presents some high-level lessons and recommendations based on the author's measurement experience.

Part IV contains some supporting material that can help the user to develop a fuller understanding of software measurement. It includes recommended readings, a review of basic statistical concepts, and some details of measurement results discussed in the earlier parts.

2

Software Engineering Data Collection

This chapter answers the question: What data (or measures) should be collected by the measurement practitioner? The answer depends on the intended use of the measures (see Parts II and III), as well as the nature of the object and attributes to be measured (discussed in Chap. 1). Appendix D reviews some other considerations of measurement scale, data collection methods, data validation, and analysis techniques. The reader who hasn't thought in statistical terms for a while may want to review this material.

The highlights of this chapter are the descriptions of two different software engineering data bases—one for research (Sec. 2-1), the other for management (Sec. 2-2)—and a recommendation for a basic set of measures for all software development organizations (Sec. 2-3). The distinction between the data bases is important. Although all software enterprises need measures for management and engineering, most don't conduct basic research.

Measurement is a basic tool of engineering, and statistical analysis is a basic tool of the experimental sciences. However, collecting and analyzing measures do not make software development an engineering or scientific discipline. Application of established measures, not analysis of potentially useful measurement approaches, characterizes engineering. Measures only become accepted and applied by practitioners when a sufficient foundation of empirical evidence accumulates, as has occurred in software cost estimation (e.g., [10]). Thus, Parts II and III of this book spend a lot of time validating the measures presented in this chapter.

2-1 A SOFTWARE DESIGN RESEARCH DATA BASE

This book's conclusions derive in part from the results of more than three years' study of a software design data base containing detailed information about eight medium-scale projects. Projects similar in terms of environment, application, and personnel were selected for study. Because of these projects' overall similarity, observed differences in cost and quality could safely be attributed to differences in system structure and development method.

Definition of Terms

Table 2-1 shows summary measures from the software design data base. Note that together these projects represent more than 2,000 modules produced by about 50 different programmers. Although this data base has many limitations, it was the largest assembly of detailed design information available to the author.

Before going on, let's define some important terms used in the table and elsewhere in this book. These definitions are largely consistent with accepted standards and usage:

- *Delivered lines of code*—counts all lines of source code delivered to the customer, including high-level language, assembler, JCL, and so on.
- *Developed lines of code*—counts all newly developed source lines of code plus 20 percent of reused lines of code [15]. This measure compensates for the lower cost and error rate attributable to reused code.
- *Delivered source instructions*—counts all noncomment source lines of code.
- *Errors*—conceptual mistakes in specification, design, or implementation. An error may result in one or more faults. Errors are recorded during integration and system testing (after unit testing).
- *Faults*—disjoint locations in the source code or documents, requiring change to fix an error. (As used here, faults are equivalent to "defects.")
- *Effort*—all hours of work charged to a project by programmers, managers, and support personnel.
- *Productivity*—developed lines of code divided by effort.
- *Unit cost*—programmer hours for unit design, code, and unit test attributed to an individual module (unit).
- *Error rate*—total errors divided by developed lines of code.
- *Fault rate*—faults attributed to a module (unit) divided by the number of executable statements in that module.

TABLE 2-1. PROJECT CHARACTERISTICS

PROJECT	TOTAL MODULES	PERCENT REUSED[a]	SIZE (KDLOC[b])	PERCENT MATHEMATICAL	ERROR RATE[c]	PRODUCTIVITY[d]
A	158	11	50	19	8.7	3.5
B	203	34	49	33	8.0	2.9
C	338	32	106	32	4.5	4.7
D	259	84	37	32	4.0	4.7
E	327	24	83	22	4.5	4.8
F	393	47	79	27	7.1	4.1
G	199	49	57	33	7.2	2.7[e]
H	245	43	56	32	6.6	2.8[e]

[a] PERCENT OF TOTAL MODULES.
[b] THOUSANDS OF DEVELOPED LINES OF CODE.
[c] ERRORS PER KDLOC.
[d] DEVELOPED LINES OF CODE PER HOUR.
[e] EXCLUDES IV&V EFFORT.

Within an organization, it is more important to measure *consistently* than to select the "right" size measure (like source lines, source instructions, or executable statements). The author's experience indicates that within a particular environment and application type, the ratios of executable statements to source lines and delivered source instructions remain fairly constant.

Because of its adoption by cost model developers, delivered source instructions may be most useful for comparison with other organizations. However, those organizations that develop extensive in-line documentation (like prologs, PDL, and comments) often prefer counting all source lines of code because that measure captures this work.

Note from the list of definitions that the measures used at the system (project) level (e.g., errors) differ from those used at the module (unit) level (e.g., faults). The data extracted for study by the author included detailed structure, cost, and error measures at both the system and module (or unit) levels. A module is the smallest unit of independently compilable code. In FORTRAN (the language used most in the projects for which data were available), a module corresponds to a subroutine. A system contains many modules, usually organized into functional subsystems.

Software Engineering Laboratory Data

The early (previously published) parts of this work were sponsored by the Software Engineering Laboratory (SEL) [16] and used a subset of its large data base. SEL is a research program sponsored by NASA Goddard Space Flight Center (GSFC). The objectives of SEL are to measure the process of software development in the flight dynamics environment at GSFC, identify technology improvements, and transition this technology to flight dynamics practitioners. Computer Sciences Corporation (CSC) provides data management, analysis, software, and documentation support to the SEL. The University of Maryland also conducts research using the SEL data base.

The SEL data base provides information on more than 50 software projects. From this set, eight similar projects (for which detailed data were available) were selected for this particular study. All the projects studied were ground-based attitude determination systems for spacecraft in near-earth orbit. The systems were developed largely by CSC for GSFC.

All eight systems were implemented in FORTRAN to run on IBM mainframe computers. All employed a common user interface and file input/output package. All systems included telemetry processing, data reduction, and attitude computation functions. Although functionally similar, the systems varied substantially in terms of specific capabilities and organization. This allowed significant differences in system design approach. The variation in system size shown in Table 2-1 provides an indication of the variability in system composition.

Sources of software design-related data included forms, documents, source code, and computer accounting. Figure 2-1 shows where these data were extracted from the software development cycle. Note that the SEL life cycle (in Fig. 2-1) does not correspond exactly to the life cycle used throughout the rest of this book.

Special forms were used to collect cost and error data directly from the software developers. The cost data were verified against time card reports. A library management system provided module change data to verify error reports. A design

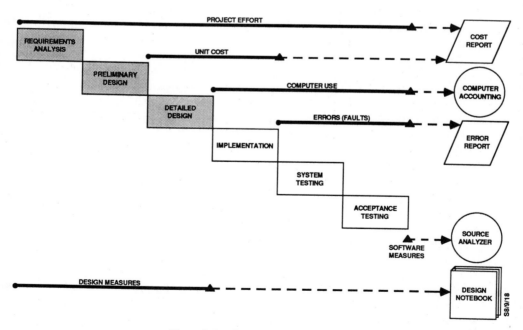

Figure 2-1. Sources of software measures

materials library was established to assemble formal design documents, notebooks, and review materials from the eight systems. A source analyzer program extracted detailed data from the source code of each system. Accounting reports provided tallies of computer use.

Because a complete set of design materials could not be recovered for all of the projects studied, many parts of this study relied on design product data derived from the software source code. The results of most design decisions are eventually reflected in the software source, but the iterative nature of the design process cannot be captured in this manner. The design data extracted from the code by the analyzer program include calling trees and counts of statements, variables, decisions, and the like. With the use of all these means, several hundred different measures were collected from each project. By the end of the study, however, only a relatively few measures had proved themselves to be really useful.

2-2 A SOFTWARE MANAGEMENT DATA BASE

CSC also maintains a management data base of large projects (separate from SEL, although there are a few projects in common). This management data base captures basic measures of cost, product, and quality at major project milestones. It provides the data necessary to develop accurate cost estimates and monitor trends in organizational performance. However, in order to provide these data at the milestones, projects must keep a continuous record of performance between milestones as well. As Fig. 2–2 shows, this results in two levels of data collection and use within the organization: the project and the enterprise.

At CSC, the Product Assurance Department is charged with collecting, maintaining, and analyzing software engineering data on a regular basis for individual projects. Product assurance officers (PAOs) are assigned to all major projects. The director of software process and measurement manages the enterprise data base (consisting of dates from all projects), and conducts training for PAOs and managers.

A production organization does not have the luxury of a research group to collect information that may or may not be useful in the future. Moreover, it is the feedback to the production organization that makes data collection worthwhile. Managers cannot act on raw data alone. Processing a large volume of data takes longer, meaning that analysis results may arrive too late to influence the course of the project. As much as possible, analysis and feedback should occur at the project level.

2-3 THE BASIC MEASUREMENT PROGRAM

The measurement needs of practitioners and researchers differ in important ways. This section presents an approach to measurement for practitioners, based on experience in a specific environment. This approach emphasizes two lessons from prac-

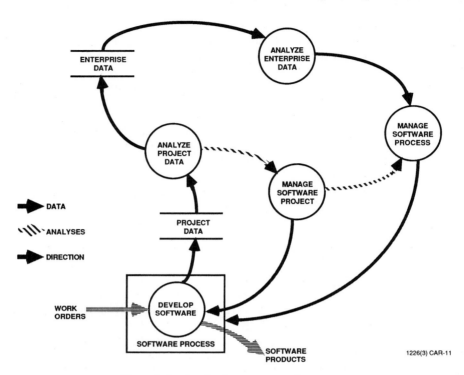

Figure 2-2. Levels of management data

tice: (1) Focus on a few key (quality) characteristics rather than attempt to measure everything, and (2) rely on simple measures extractable from common design products (and other sources). Many measurement schemes (e.g., those advanced by McCall [5] and DeMarco [11]) require more detail than is practical for the typical software enterprise. The leap from zero or a few measures to several hundred is too big to take at once.

Figure 2-3 shows the basic set of measures recommended here. It covers essential cost, quality, and product attributes. The data items in the figure are "metric primitives" (as used by DeMarco [11]). They can be combined in many useful ways to form rates and percentages. Later chapters explain the measures of Fig. 2-3 in more detail and provide reasons for the selection of these specific measures and not others.

Although design is the focus of this measurement set, the entire development cycle is covered to some extent in Fig. 2-3. (One of DeMarco's laws [11] states that costs migrate from anything that is measured to something that is not.) Most organizations will eventually want to collect more data than this (in particular, COCOMO type [10] personnel and technology factors), but it provides a good starting point. Measurement must be a long-term activity. A single data point is of lim-

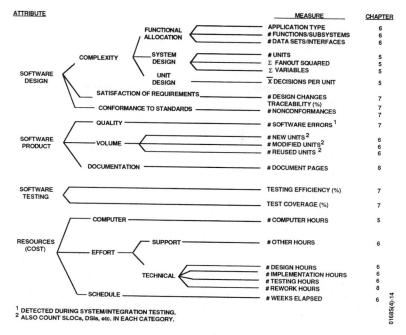

ATTRIBUTE			MEASURE	CHAPTER

SOFTWARE DESIGN
- COMPLEXITY
  - FUNCTIONAL ALLOCATION
    - APPLICATION TYPE — 6
    - # FUNCTIONS/SUBSYSTEMS — 6
    - # DATA SETS/INTERFACES — 6
  - SYSTEM DESIGN
    - # UNITS — 5
    - Σ FANOUT SQUARED — 5
    - Σ VARIABLES — 5
  - UNIT DESIGN
    - $\overline{X}$ DECISIONS PER UNIT — 5
- SATISFACTION OF REQUIREMENTS
  - # DESIGN CHANGES — 7
  - TRACEABILITY (%) — 7
- CONFORMANCE TO STANDARDS
  - # NONCONFORMANCES — 7

SOFTWARE PRODUCT
- QUALITY — # SOFTWARE ERRORS [1] — 7
- VOLUME
  - # NEW UNITS [2] — 6
  - # MODIFIED UNITS [2] — 6
  - # REUSED UNITS [2] — 6
- DOCUMENTATION — # DOCUMENT PAGES — 8

SOFTWARE TESTING
- TESTING EFFICIENCY (%) — 7
- TEST COVERAGE (%) — 7

RESOURCES (COST)
- COMPUTER — # COMPUTER HOURS — 5
- EFFORT
  - SUPPORT — # OTHER HOURS — 6
  - TECHNICAL
    - # DESIGN HOURS — 6
    - # IMPLEMENTATION HOURS — 6
    - # TESTING HOURS — 6
    - # REWORK HOURS — 8
- SCHEDULE — # WEEKS ELAPSED — 6

[1] DETECTED DURING SYSTEM/INTEGRATION TESTING.
[2] ALSO COUNT SLOCs, DSIs, etc. IN EACH CATEGORY.

0168S(4)-14

Figure 2-3. Basic software measurement set

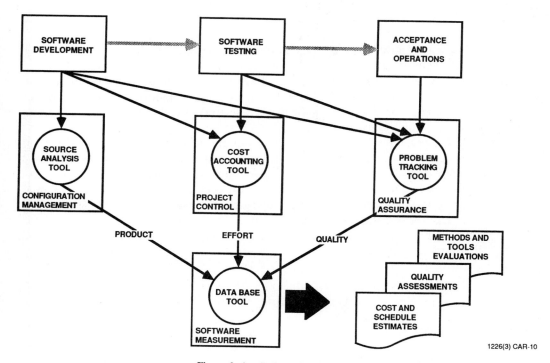

1226(3) CAR-10

Figure 2-4. Software data collection system

ited use. Measurement provides a systematic way of learning from past experience and applying that learning to current activities. Over time, a measurement program must evolve to satisfy organizational needs.

Most organizations have structures in place that can help to collect these data. Figure 2–4 shows that configuration management, project control, and quality assurance elements have access to most of the data an enterprise needs. Common tools like line counters, librarians, and project management systems can minimize the cost of data collection. Design data can be captured by workstations. For example, CSC's Design Generator* implements the design measurement and analysis scheme explained in more detail in Chap. 5.

Still, nothing is free. DeMarco [11] estimates the cost of his measurement program at 5 to 10 percent of software development costs. SEL experience indicates that data collection and processing costs range from 7 to 8 percent [17]. Because the recommended measures of Fig. 2–3 are an order of magnitude fewer than either the DeMarco or the SEL program, their cost should be less than 1 percent of software development cost. That amount can easily be justified as recapturable through improved performance and better management visibility into the software process. Compared to the 5 to 15 percent cost of a typical inspection-based product assurance program, measurement is an inexpensive addition to software development.

2-4 SUMMARY

This chapter proposed a measurement approach based on a small initial set of key measures. That proposal developed from actual measurement experience in a software production environment. Most organizations will find it easier to implement this limited, low-cost approach than to implement more elaborate ones. Most organizations already have structures in place that could facilitate the data collection process.

Part II describes what has been learned about using the basic measurement set to assess software design quality. In particular, Chap. 5 describes a model of software design complexity and modularity, demonstrates the empirical evidence supporting it, and shows how engineers can use the model to analyze designs. Because different design steps employ different processes of mentation and produce different forms of notation, complexity measures differ from step to step. Part III explains how managers can use design and other software measures to estimate costs, control quality, and evaluate technology.

---

*Design Generator is a registered trademark of Computer Sciences Corporation.

3

Software Complexity Measures

Concern for software measurement is at least as old as software engineering. Although significant work has been done in the area, Redwine and Riddle [18] report that measurement technology is still one of the most immature in the field of software engineering. In spite of many individual achievements, as yet no common framework integrating these individual measurement approaches has emerged. This book synthesizes such a structure for design measurement (in Chap. 5) from the diverse results obtained to date, some of which are reviewed in this and the following chapter.

Many attempts have been made to quantify software complexity in particular. Curtis [19] identifies two basic views of complexity, computational and cognitive. The first deals with machine efficiency; the latter addresses human issues of difficulty and understandability. As indicated in Chap. 1, this book focuses on the effects of cognitive complexity on software produceability. If the programmer is more likely to make mistakes and/or take a long time to implement a complex design, then complexity measures can provide a basis for figures of merit for design quality.

Along these lines, researchers have proposed a plethora of software and design complexity measures. Unfortunately, most such proposals lack any substantial empirical evidence of their value. The most frequently published argument for the validity of a new measure is that it agrees with other previously published (but usually not substantiated) measures. Most empirical data come from experiments performed with college students. However, such results cannot be counted on to scale up in a production environment.

Curtis [19] characterizes the state of measurement validation thusly: "For every positive validation there is a negative validation." This ambiguity about measurement evaluation means that the store of software measurement ideas increases daily. Measures persist even when challenged by evidence and experience. A quick review of two major measurement schemes, software science and cyclomatic complexity, illustrates some of the problems that arise in developing and evaluating measures.

3-1 SOFTWARE SCIENCE

Halstead [20] made the first major formal effort to distinguish software science from computer science. He concentrated on the analogy between programming languages and natural languages. Although Halstead's work was done at the code level rather than design, its impact on software measurement has been so great that it deserves special mention.

Starting with the notion that the "minimal representation" of a program consists of a function with associated input/output operands, Halstead developed a system of equations predicting program size, effort, errors, and so on. Operators and operands form the basic units of measurement in software science. An operator (like a verb) establishes or changes the value or relationship between operands. An operand can be any data item, a variable or constant (like a noun). The set of different operators and operands constitutes the vocabulary of a program. Figure 3-1 shows a sample FORTRAN program; Fig. 3-2 identifies the operators and operands in the program. The sample program has a total of 16 unique operators and 21 unique operands.

Table 3-1 shows how Halstead related counts of operators and operands to properties of programs. The essential premise of software science is that any programming task consists of selecting and arranging a finite number of program components (operators and operands). The number of these components then determines the implementation effort required and the number of errors produced, as shown in Table 3-1. At the time, Halstead did not provide any rigorous justification for the derivation of these equations.

Software science has proved to be more controversial than any other measurement scheme; since its publication, it has been criticized on many fronts. Malenge [21] presented a thorough review, finding several errors in methodology, especially in the use of logarithmic transformations. Coulter [22] focused on the incorrect use of human memory models. Lister [23] and Hamer and Frewin [24] criticized the experimental methods. Shen et al. [25] pointed out the questionable derivation of some software science equations.

```
100          SUBROUTINE TDIST (N, X, Y, DIST)
200C                                                    PASSED
300          INTEGER   N
400          REAL      X(N), Y(N), DIST
500C                                                    LOCAL
600          INTEGER   I, MSGNUM, K
700          REAL      XL, YL, DX, DY, X2, Y2, R2, R
800          LOGICAL   ERR
900C                                                    GLOBAL
1000         REAL      SQRT
1100C                                                   INITIALIZE
1200         XL = 0.0
1300         YL = 0.0
1400         DIST = 0.0
1500C                                                   FOR ALL POINTS
1600         DO 200 I=1, N
1700           DX = X(I) - XL
1800           X2 = DX*DX
1900           DY = Y(I) - YL
2000           Y2 = DY*DY
2100C                                                   CALC./CHECK SEPARATION
2200           R2 = X2 + Y2
2300           CALL VERIFY (R2, ERR)
2400C                                                   OBTAIN SEPARATION
2500           IF (ERR) THEN
2600             K = I - 1
2700             WRITE (6, 100, ERR=300) K, I
2800     100     FORMAT (1X, 'ERROR, POINTS ', I3, ' AND ', I3,
2900      *              ' TOO CLOSE')
3000             R = 0.0
3100           ELSE
3200             R = SORT (R2)
3300           END IF
3400C                                                   ACCUMULATE
3500           DIST = DIST + R
3600           XL = X(I)
3700           YL = Y(I)
3800     200 CONTINUE
3900C                                                   NORMAL RETURN
4000         RETURN
4100C                                                   ERROR WRITING MESSAGE
4200     300 CONTINUE
4300         MSGNUM = 27
4400         CALL ERRMSG (MSGNUM, *400)
4500         RETURN
4600C                                                   UNABLE TO WRITE ANY
4700C                                                   MESSAGES, ABORT RUN
4800     400 CONTINUE
4900         CALL ABORT
5000C
5100         END
```

Figure 3-1. Sample FORTRAN program

SAMPLE.FOR/HL/DB/SL/XP

HALSTEAD OPERATORS

.DELIMETERS

0 //	0 **	3 *	0 /	2 +	3 =
15 =	5 (	2 ,	0 &	0 .NE.	0 .LT.
0 .LE.	0 .EQ.	0 .GE.	0 .GT.	0 .AND.	0 .OR.
0 .XOR.	0 .EQV.	0 .NOT.	0 .NEQV.		

KEYWORDS

0 IF()	0 IF(),,	1 .IF()	0 ELSE IF	1 ELSE	1 DO=,,
0 DOWHILE	0 ASSIGNTO	20 EOS			

PROCEDURES

1 VERIFY	1 SORT	1 ERRMSG	1 ABORT

TRANSFERS

1 ERR=	300	
1 ALT.RET.	ERRMSG	400

HALSTEAD OPERANDS

2 1	6 I	1 K	1 N	3 B	2 X	2 Y	1 27
3 R2	2 X2	2 Y2	4 0.0	1 300	1 400	3 DX	3 DY
3 XL	3 YL	2 ERR	3 DIST	4 MSGNUM			

Figure 3-2. Tabulation of operators and operands

TABLE 3-1. SOFTWARE SCIENCE RELATIONSHIPS

QUALITY	EQUATION
VOCABULARY (n)	$n = n_1 + n_2$
LENGTH (N)	$N = N_1 + N_2$
VOLUME (V)	$V = N \log_2 n$
LEVEL (L)	$L = V/V^*$
EFFORT (E)	$E = V/L$
FAULTS (B)	$B = V/S^*$

S8/9/14

NOTES: V* IS THE MINIMUM VOLUME REPRESENTED BY A BUILT-IN
FUNCTION PERFORMING THE TASK OF THE ENTIRE PROGRAM.

S* IS THE MEAN NUMBER OF MENTAL DISCRIMINATIONS
(DECISIONS) BETWEEN ERRORS (S* ≃ 3000).

NUMBER OF UNIQUE OPERATORS (n_1), e.g., +, −, IF

NUMBER OF UNIQUE OPERANDS (n_2), e.g., X, Y, I, 200

TOTAL NUMBER OF APPEARANCES OF OPERATORS (N_1)

TOTAL NUMBER OF APPEARANCES OF OPERANDS (N_2)

Advocates of software science argue that empirical data support it [26], in spite of theoretical objections. Attempts to validate Halstead's software science measures have followed two approaches: internal validation of length and volume correspondences and external validation of effort and error predictions (see Table 3-1). The following sections highlight some specific objections in each of these areas. These results suggest that software science measures are more important because of the approach they represent than because of their usefulness in practice.

Length and Volume

Most of the empirical support for software science, per se, comes from analyses of the relationship between estimated and actual length. Halstead [20] proposed that the actual length of a program could be estimated with the following equation:

$$\tilde{N} = n_1 \log_2 n_1 + n_2 \log_2 n_2 \qquad (3-1)$$

where

$$\tilde{N} = \text{estimated program length}$$
$$n_1 = \text{number of unique operators}$$
$$n_2 = \text{number of unique operands}$$

The $\log_2$ function results from Halstead's often criticized model of how programmers select and combine operators and operands. Malenge [21] describes this program length formula as "the basic relation of software [science]."

Researchers have reported discovering correlations as high as 0.95 between the actual (N) and predicted ($\tilde{N}$) length of programs [26]. However, Card and Agresti [27] show that these correlations cannot be accepted at face value because N and $\tilde{N}$ are mathematically dependent under the conditions that are obtained in actual programs. Both are functions of n_1 and n_2, so a correlation exists by definition. This study demonstrates that the length equation lacks empirical as well as theoretical support for its internal relations.

Effort and Errors

Ostensibly, software science provides equations for estimating the effort (cost) and errors of developed software (see Table 3–1), key indicators of produceability. Halstead's formulas for effort and bugs suggest they depend only on the volume of tokens processed by the programmer, not on the "complexity" of relationships among tokens. Thus, it should not be surprising that the software science measures do not perform any better as estimators than simple size measures like source lines of code.

Table 3–2 shows some results obtained by Basili [28]. The table reports correlations of various measures with counts of errors and hours (not rates). Conclusion: Larger products require more hours of effort and have more errors, regardless of how size is measured.

Researchers have had more success in using individual software science ideas than in using the theory as a whole. For example, Albrecht and Gaffney [29] have used operands as input to function point and software size estimation algorithms.

Although it represents a milestone in software measurement theory, *practitioners can safely ignore software science* at present. It probably represents the wrong level of detail for most measurement applications; designers and programmers do not think in terms of individual operators and operands.

TABLE 3–2. PREDICTING EFFORT AND ERRORS USING SIZE AND COMPLEXITY METRICS

MEASURE	CORRELATION COEFFICIENT	
	EFFORT	ERRORS
CALLS	0.80	0.57
CYCLOMATIC COMPLEXITY	0.74	0.56
LINES OF CODE	0.76	0.56
EXECUTABLE STATEMENTS	0.74	0.55
REVISIONS	0.71	0.67
HALSTEAD EFFORT	0.66	0.54

ADAPTED FROM V.R. BASILI, "EVALUATING SOFTWARE DEVELOPMENT CHARACTERISTICS: ASSESSMENT OF SOFTWARE MEASURES IN THE SOFTWARE ENGINEERING LABORATORY," <u>PROCEEDINGS OF SIXTH ANNUAL SOFTWARE ENGINEERING WORKSHOP</u>, SEL-81-013, DECEMBER 1981

3-2 CYCLOMATIC COMPLEXITY

Another well-developed concept of measurement, cyclomatic complexity, was introduced by McCabe [30] to quantify control flow complexity. McCabe's original objectives were to determine the number of paths through a program that must be tested to ensure complete coverage and to rate the difficulty of understanding a program. Because of its intuitive appeal, other researchers have attempted to relate cyclomatic complexity to error rate and cost too.

Cyclomatic complexity derives from the graphic representation of a program's control flow. Figure 3–3 represents the control flow of the sample program from Fig. 3–1. Each node in the graph corresponds to a decision or target in the program.

The cyclomatic number of the program equals the number of disjoint regions defined by the graph. For a fully connected graph, the cyclomatic number is the number of binary decisions plus one. The sample program of Fig. 3–1 (as repre-

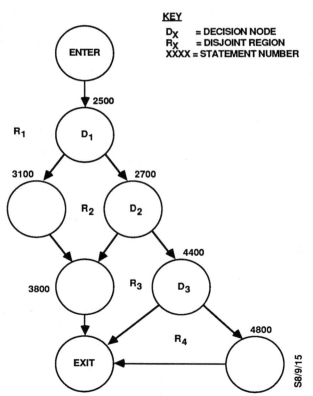

KEY
D_X = DECISION NODE
R_X = DISJOINT REGION
XXXX = STATEMENT NUMBER

S8/9/15

Figure 3–3. Graphic representation of cyclomatic complexity (for program in Fig. 3–1)

sented in Fig. 3–3) has a cyclomatic number of four. McCabe's [30] general formula for cyclomatic complexity is

$$V(G) = e - n + 2p \qquad (3\text{–}2)$$

where

$V(G)$ = cyclomatic number of graph G
e = number of edges
n = number of nodes
p = number of unconnected parts

McCabe [30] suggested that, in order to promote testability and understandability, no program (module) should exceed a cyclomatic complexity of ten.

Cyclomatic complexity has been an active area of both research and practical application almost since its inception. (Gilb [31] proposed another measurement scheme similarly based on counts of decisions.) Myers [32] extended McCabe's theory to include decisions based on compound conditions. Evangelist [33] suggested reformulation to more completely reflect control flow. Hansen [34] proposed a hybrid measure incorporating cyclomatic complexity and software science measures. Currently, many testing experts recommend use of the cyclomatic representation to ensure adequate test coverage.

In spite of some initial favorable indications, efforts to extend cyclomatic complexity to predict the software error rate have met with limited success. Again, as Table 3–2 shows, cyclomatic complexity did not do any better in this regard than did gross measures like source lines of code. Nevertheless, cyclomatic complexity continues to be a useful measure for test planning and control. Chapter 5 will show that its understandability aspect relates to maintainability. For many measurement applications, cyclomatic complexity does represent the right level of detail; designers and programmers do think in terms of decisions.

3-3 OTHER COMPLEXITY MEASURES

Many (probably more than 100) other approaches to measuring software complexity have been proposed. These may be roughly categorized as dealing with systems of units or individual units alone (the macro view versus the micro view). Both the software science and cyclomatic complexity models fall into the micro-level category. Here are some other good examples:

1. System complexity models (macro-level)
   McClure [35]—invocation complexity
   Belady and Evangelisti [36]—system partitioning

Henry and Kafura [37]—information flow
Yau and Collofello [38]—stability
2. Unit complexity models (micro-level)
Elshoff [39]—reference span
Woodfield [40]—review complexity
Woodward et al. [41]—program knots

Obviously, space does not permit full individual discussions of all these models. However, some remarks are in order even at the risk of overgenerality.

Researchers and practitioners assume that macro-level measures are more appropriate for cost estimation because they are less sensitive to variations in individual programmer performance and development methods. Software standards, for example, can strongly influence micro-level measures like decisions per module and program knots. (A knot is a place where lines of control cross. Knots are departures from proper program structure.) Precisely because they respond to these variations, micro-level measures are assumed to relate most strongly to software characteristics like understandability.

However, none of these models provided a usable measure of design quality due to one or more of the following difficulties: (1) Necessary measures could not be extracted from the SEL data base, (2) required information would not, in any event, be available during design (a special problem with the micro-level models), or (3) SEL data did not support the model. Many of these measures do not do any better than simple lines-of-code measures at predicting cost or error rate.

Nevertheless, as discussed in Chap. 5 many of these measurement ideas were successfully incorporated into a design complexity model. In particular, the model relies on concepts from McClure [35], Belady and Evangelisti [36], Henry and Kafura [37], and McCabe [30].

3-4 SUMMARY

This chapter reviewed the measurement schemes of software science and cyclomatic complexity. Empirical evidence suggests that although cyclomatic complexity has practical applications, software science, per se, does not. Many other measurement approaches have been developed at both the system (macro) level and unit (micro) level, but the evidence regarding them is inconclusive.

The macro-level models generally attempt to relate complexity to modularity (or interconnectivity), the way in which units are defined and interact. However modularity, itself, is subject to differing interpretations. Chapter 4 focuses on the notion of modularity, how it can be measured and its effect on produceability.

4

Design Modularization Heuristics

Design methods provide rules for system construction but generally do not identify corresponding measures of quality. Nevertheless, many design measures have evolved in association with design heuristics (rules for developing good systems). In practice, specifying quality objectives like modularity and simplicity does not ensure quality products unless more specific guidance is given. That guidance often takes the form of software standards and rules of thumb.

Perhaps the most widely accepted quality objective for design is modularity. The approach of designing modular systems attempts to produce individual modules (or units) that are as self-contained and independent of each other as possible. This means limiting both data and control connections among modules. Modularity (in terms of strength/cohesion and coupling, defined below) is the principal objective of structured design [42]. Parnas's principle of information hiding [43] provides another strategy for modularization based on limiting the scope of changes.

Heuristics attempt to capture underlying design principles. For example, module strength/cohesion measures "singleness of purpose." A module performing only a single function has the greatest strength. A module performing several unrelated functions has low strength. Module coupling measures "dependence" between modules. Two modules linked only through data passed in a calling sequence have the weakest coupling. The use of control flags and COMMON blocks increases the level of coupling. Myers [44] argues that software quality can be improved by maximizing module strength and minimizing module coupling.

This chapter reviews the evidence regarding some common design heuristics for achieving modularity. They are widely assumed to contribute to produceability. These heuristics recommend

- Small modules
- Limited data coupling
- Medium span of control
- Singleness of purpose

Constructing measures corresponding to the heuristics makes it possible to evaluate their effectiveness. For example, the "7 ± 2 rule" for span of control states that each module should have from five to nine subordinate modules (medium span of control) or no subordinate modules at all. This rule defines a measure and specifies a range of acceptable values for it.

A valid heuristic will show a favorable effect on produceability. Then the measure corresponding to a valid heuristic provides a simple criterion for evaluating that aspect of software design quality. Analyzing actual measurement data enables the researcher to prove, disprove, or improve the underlying heuristic.

4-1 MODULE SIZE

One simple approach to promoting modularity is tc limit module size in terms of executable statements or another measure of program length (e.g., Halstead length [20]; see Chap. 3). Many programming texts suggest limiting module size to one page (or 50 to 60 source lines of code). Military standards for module size range from 50 to 200 executable statements. Such standards are easy to define and enforce, but their real contribution to software quality remains unclear.

Most empirical studies of module size begin with a graph like Fig. 4–1 showing the relationship between module size and error rate. Analysts often fit a straight or curved line to the data to show a decreasing fault rate with increasing size (contradicting the conventional wisdom that smaller modules are better). However, this approach ignores the underlying distribution of the data (see Appendix D). A small module can have only zero faults or a high fault rate (when measured as faults per executable statement). Note the empty triangular space in the lower left corner of Fig. 4–1.

Looking at these data from a nonparametric perspective leads to a different conclusion [45]. Table 4–1 shows the results of dividing 453 modules (from Fig. 4–1) into three size classes. Note that relative cyclomatic complexity (mean decisions per executable statement) is about the same for all classes. Table 4–1 also reports two different fault rate statistics for the three classes of module size. The mean fault

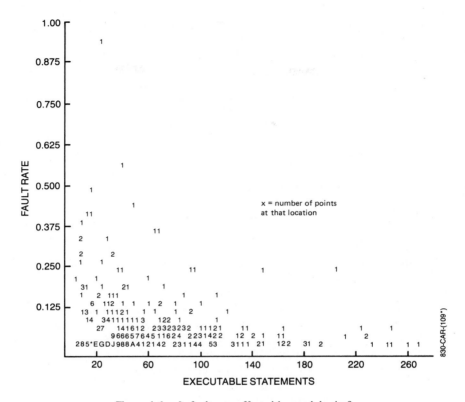

Figure 4-1.   Is fault rate affected by module size?

rate declines with increasing module size, supporting the usual interpretation of Fig. 4-1. But the more conservative measure, the median fault rate, tells a different story. More than half of all small modules do not exhibit any fault at all.

Which are more reliable, large or small modules? To answer this question, look at Table 4-2. It shows a cross-tabulation of module size class by fault rate class. A test of the nonparametric gamma correlation coefficient indicates that no

TABLE 4-1.   MODULE CHARACTERISTICS BY SIZE CLASS

MODULE SIZE	NUMBER OF FORTRAN MODULES	EXECUTABLE STATEMENTS	MEAN DECISIONS PER EXECUTABLE STATEMENT	FAULT RATE	
				MEAN	MEDIAN
SMALL	154	1 TO 31	0.31	0.063	0.000
MEDIUM	148	32 TO 64	0.31	0.051	0.024
LARGE	151	65 OR MORE	0.32	0.038	0.021

TABLE 4-2. CONTINGENCY TABLE ANALYSIS SHOWS MODULE SIZE AND FAULT RATE INDEPENDENT

SIZE	FAULT RATE		
	ZERO	**MEDIUM**	**HIGH**
SMALL	90	9	55
MEDIUM	50	55	43
LARGE	32	78	41

TOTAL MODULES = 453
GAMMA (γ) **= 0.20**

relationship exists between fault rate and module size. Note that almost all small modules have either no faults or a high fault rate.

Table 4-2 shows that although the distribution of fault rate for small modules differs from that of large modules, we cannot conclude that there is a consistent trend. (A trend is indicated when the largest values in each column all lie along the same diagonal.) *Thus, module size, per se, does not affect fault rate.* An analysis by Takahashi and Kamayachi [46] of data from 30 software development projects also showed that program size in terms of source lines of code did not exhibit any strong relationship to error rate. In their study, programmer experience proved to be the best predictor of error rate.

On the other hand, module cost in terms of hours per executable statement does appear to be related to module size. Figure 4-2 shows the distribution of cost for the three size classes. The percentages shown derive from a cross-tabulation like that shown in Table 4-2. The results indicate that *larger modules cost less (per executable statement) than smaller ones.*

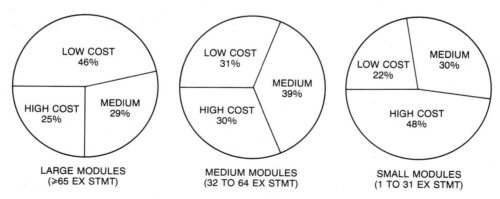

Figure 4-2. Large modules tend to cost less per executable statement to develop

Some savings come from distributing the interface definition and prolog costs over a larger number of executable statements. However, a part of these savings could be lost again owing to increased testing requirements.

4-2 DATA COUPLING

Two modules share a data couple when data flow from one to the other or are shared in a global (common) area. Myers [44] defines six levels of data coupling. Ordered from best to worst, they are (simple) data, stamp, control, external, common, and content coupling. A study [45] compared common coupling with higher levels of coupling achieved through passing variables in argument lists. Some authors argue against any common coupling, in spite of the potential for long and unwieldy argument lists in some situations. Others object on structured programming grounds.

For this analysis [45], modules were grouped into three ordered classes with respect to the percentage of (externally defined) referenced variables that appeared in COMMON: zero, ≤ 15 percent, and > 15 percent. A module with zero referenced variables in COMMON passed all input/output through the argument list (or uncounted read/write operations).

No relationship was observed when fault rate and coupling type were cross-classified (see Table 4–2 for an example). Figure 4–3 presents the results of the cross-classification graphically. *The distribution of error rate does not depend on the coupling mechanism.* Another similar study [47] failed to show any significant difference between global and parameter coupling with respect to modifiability.

Earlier recommendations that common coupling was best avoided were based on experience before the general availability of INCLUDE processors. In an environment where only a single version of a COMMON block definition needs to be maintained, common coupling is an acceptable, and sometimes preferable, alternative to parameter coupling. This result highlights the dependence of effective soft-

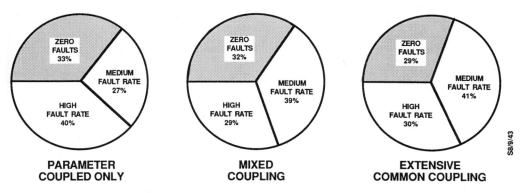

Figure 4–3. Fault rate not influenced by coupling type

ware engineering practice on the state of computer and systems technology. Continual change in this infrastructure requires periodic reexamination of software methodologies and standards.

4-3 SPAN OF CONTROL

When one module invokes (calls) another module, it establishes a control couple between the two modules. The number of other modules invoked by a given module defines its span of control. Many different heuristics for span of control exist. Structured design texts discourage modules with a span of control of just one, arguing that a module that calls just one other might as well include that module's function in itself. Variations of the 7 ± 2 rule suggest seven as the maximum span of control, or alternatively, that the span of control should range from 5 to 9.

In an effort to evaluate these heuristics, a study [45] grouped modules into three ordered classes with respect to span of control: one, two to seven, and more than seven. Terminal nodes (no descendants) were excluded from analysis. Span of control was cross-classified with fault rate and development cost (see Table 4-2 for an example). The results indicated that *modules with larger spans of control tend to cost more* (gamma = 0.25) *and have a higher fault rate* (gamma = 0.33). The probability of these correlations being due to chance is less than 0.01.

Figure 4-4 illustrates the magnitude of the difference in fault rate among span of control classes. Only 12 percent of modules with more than seven descendants were fault-free, whereas 42 percent of modules with exactly one descendant were fault-free. Apparently, the smaller the span of control, the better. Encapsulating even a single well-defined function (resulting in a fanout of one) is good design practice. Troy and Zweben [48] obtained similar results using this measure of modularity.

Curtis [19] suggests that the 7 ± 2 rule developed from a misunderstanding of

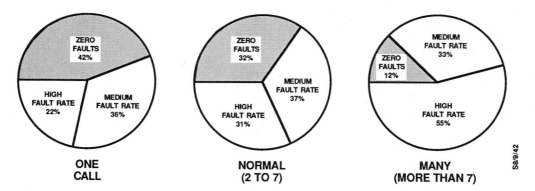

Figure 4-4. Fault rate decreases with decrease in span of control

certain psychological results. It actually refers to retention of simple stimuli. Each call (or invocation) is actually a complex structure involving several data items and control relationships. A single call could easily exceed the 7 ± 2 limit of simple stimuli.

4-4 MODULE STRENGTH/COHESION

The concept of module strength or cohesion refers to the relationship among the elements of a module (subprogram). Ideally, all the elements of a module should contribute to performing a single well-defined function. Myers [44] defines seven levels of module strength. In descending order, these are functional, informational, communicational, procedural, classical, logical, and coincidental. A high-strength (functional) module performs a single function. A low-strength (coincidental) module includes multiple unrelated functions. Myers contends that high-strength modules are better than low-strength ones.

Although some recent attempts to develop objective measures of module strength seem promising conceptually, the proposed measures are not easily extracted from common design materials. (Chapter 5 describes an indirect measure.) The lack of an appropriate objective design measure has hindered studies of the module strength/cohesion heuristic.

One study [45] relied on a subjective assessment of module strength/cohesion. Programmers determined the strength of modules via a checklist, rating each module they developed as performing one or more of the following funtions: input/output, logic/control, and/or algorithmic processing. More different function types means less singleness of purpose. Those modules described as having only one type of function were classified as high strength; those having two types, medium strength; and those having three types, low strength. Table 4–3 summarizes the results of this classification process.

A cross-tabulation of module strength with fault rate showed a correlation (gamma) of -0.35 (see Table 4–2 for an example). The probability that this correlation is due to random factors is less than 0.001. Thus, *higher strength modules tend*

TABLE 4–3.   MODULE CHARACTERISTICS BY STRENGTH/COHESION

MODULE STRENGTH	NUMBER OF FORTRAN MODULES	MEAN EXECUTABLE STATEMENTS	MEAN DECISIONS PER EXECUTABLE STATEMENT
LOW	90	77	0.29
MEDIUM	176	60	0.32
HIGH	187	48	0.32

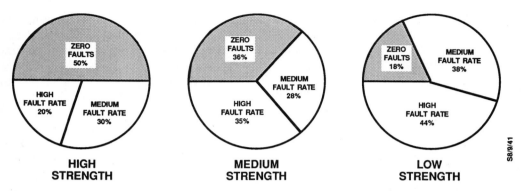

Figure 4-5. Fault rate for classes of module strength/cohesion

to have lower fault rates. Figure 4–5 provides a better picture of the strength of this relationship. Fifty percent of high-strength modules were fault-free, whereas only 18 percent of low-strength modules were fault-free. No significant relationship was discovered between module strength and development cost.

Returning to Table 4–3, note that module size decreases with increasing strength. A subsequent analysis [49] considered the possibility of an interaction between module size and strength, as well as the effects of programmer performance. Table 4–4 summarizes the results. After controlling the effect of module size, a weak but significant relationship between module strength and development cost emerges. *Higher-strength modules tend to cost less to develop.* The relationship between module strength and fault rate does not appear to be affected by module size.

Table 4–4 also shows that the correlations between module size and fault rate

TABLE 4-4. SUMMARY OF CONTINGENCY TABLE RESULTS COMPARING MODULE SIZE AND STRENGTH

CRITERIA	EFFECT CONTROLLED	CORRELATIONS[a]	
		FAULT RATE	COST RATE
MODULE STRENGTH	NONE	−0.35[b]	−0.19
	SIZE	−0.32[b]	−0.27[b]
	PROGRAMMER	−0.21	0.10
MODULE SIZE	NONE	0.20	−0.31[b]
	STRENGTH	0.19	−0.38[b]
	PROGRAMMER	0.27[b]	−0.41[b]

[a]GAMMA (γ) STATISTIC.
[b]PROBABILITY IS LESS THAN 0.001 THAT CORRELATION IS ACTUALLY ZERO.

and development cost decrease dramatically when variation in programmer performance is controlled. This result suggests that *high-strength modules are produced by the same programmers that produce low-cost, low-fault-rate modules.* Of the 26 programmers in the sample, 16 developed nine or more modules. Together these programmers accounted for 413 of the 453 modules. For each of these programmers, the percentage of zero-fault and high-strength modules was computed.

Figure 4–6 shows the relationship between percent zero fault and percent high strength by programmer. The figure shows two clusters of programmers. Those who produce low-fault-rate (high percent zero fault) modules tend to produce high-strength modules. The probability was less than 0.05 that the (Spearman) correlation coefficient of 0.53 was due to random factors. A similar analysis of percent low cost and percent high strength did not show any significant relationship.

Finding that programmer performance incorporates the relationship between module strength and fault rate does not affect its validity. Good programmers use good practices. Good software does not result from random programmer behavior. A great deal has been made of the 10 or 20 to 1 variation in programmer performance. Although everyone's limits are different, performance increases with training and the acquisition of improved methods. The notion of the "superprogrammer"

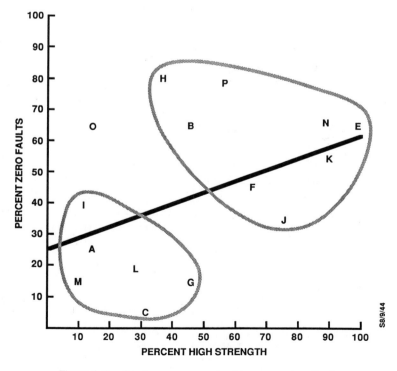

Figure 4–6. Good programmers tend to use good methods

who succeeds without any regard for good practice is a myth. Of course, that good practice may be acquired intuitively (in some cases), rather than through formal training.

Focusing solely on variations in individual programmer performance may obscure the additional goal of improving everyone's performance. Indeed, managers should pay more attention to recruiting and rewarding the best performers, but that strategy alone is inadequate over the long term, especially in view of the continuing shortage of competent personnel.

4-5 SUMMARY

This chapter explained four common design heuristics and then reviewed some studies of their effectiveness. The results of those studies are summarized in Table 4–5. The evidence suggests the need for some modifications to traditional thinking:

- Standards limiting the size of software units seem ill-advised. However, in Chap. 5 it is argued that complexity limits may promote maintainability.
- Don't denigrate common coupling. Use common or parameter coupling as appropriate to the design problem. Chapter 5 provides some criteria to help choose.
- Minimize span of control. Forget the 7 ± 2 rule. Decompose each function gradually. Chapter 5 explains a model for functional decomposition.
- Try to achieve module strength/cohesion by encapsulating each function in a separate module. However, better measures of this characteristic are needed.

Although individual performance remains the largest identifiable factor in software design quality, it is not independent of good design practice. Good designers use

TABLE 4–5. SUMMARY OF DESIGN MODULARIZATION EMPIRICAL FINDINGS

CONCEPT	EFFECT ON		TENTATIVE CONCLUSION
	COST	FAULT RATE	
Module size	Larger— costs less	No effect	There is some reason to prefer larger modules (but see strength, below)
Data coupling	No effect	No effect	Common coupling appears to be as valid as parameter coupling
Span of control (fanout)	Smaller— costs less	Smaller- fewer errors	Reduced span of control is beneficial to both cost and quality
Strength (cohesion)	Higher— costs less	Higher- fewer errors	High strength is beneficial to both cost and quality

good practices. The results also show that the effectiveness of a particular practice or heuristic can change over time as the computing environment changes.

Properly adjusted, these rules help to improve design quality. For example, results show that a design consisting of many small modules, achieved by rapid decomposition (high fanout) without regard for functionality (strength/cohesion), is a bad design. Chapter 5 presents an explanation of a model of software design quality that incorporates this information.

5

Product Engineering with Complexity Criteria

Chapters 3 and 4 outlined some of the extensive research on complexity and modularity that has been done. This chapter integrates those results and others into a general model. It explains an approach to measuring software design complexity that considers the structure of the overall system as well as the complexity incorporated in individual components. It ties the concept of modularity directly to complexity measures. The result is a set of figures of merit for design quality with respect to produceability.

The model of Fig. 5–1 represents one view of software quality. It includes two sets of quality relations that need to be considered by the designer: traceability and producibility. Achieving traceability means showing that the design satisfies the functional and performance requirements of the customer. Achieving produceability means developing a design that provides for implementability and maintainability. Produceability implies minimized cost, minimized error insertion, and maximized maintainability.

As suggested by the name, traceability can be demonstrated by tracing each requirements item to the design component that implements it. Common techniques include traceability matrices and system verification diagrams [50]. Although impor-

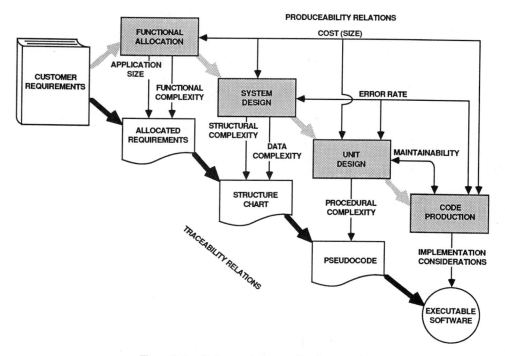

Figure 5-1.   Software design quality framework

tant topics in their own right, discussion of those techniques falls outside the scope of this book. Here, we will focus on design metrics that can help us *produce* better software.

The concept of produceability implies a system of causes and effects (see Fig. 5-1). Although all design activities interact with the produceability relations to an extent, some special interactions exist:

> Functional allocation defines the magnitude of the system to be built. That is the first cause of cost. It is not so much a first cause of errors, as a functional allocation may be incomplete or redundant, but otherwise it is hard to say it is "wrong."
>
> System design prescribes the strategy for implementing the requirements. The difficulty of that strategy determines the propensity of developers to make errors; thus, system design tends to be the first cause of errors.
>
> Unit design is the first cause of poor maintainability, as it is there that modules, a key unit of product maintenance, are designed.

Although in Fig. 5–1 we see that produceability concerns relations among design (and other) *activities,* usually only the design and code *products* can be measured directly. In the center diagonal of Fig. 5–1 we see the complexity factors manifested in these design products. Because the information available to the designer changes with each activity, different measures of design complexity are needed for each activity. This book provides for that by defining measures that are easily extractable from the products produced by each activity (i.e., system diagram, structure chart, pseudocode, and the like).

Section 5-1 presents complexity measures for each level of design. Section 5-2 describes the empirical evidence supporting this model of design complexity. Section 5-3 shows how the measures can be used for optimizing design in terms of produceability.

5-1 MODELING SOFTWARE DESIGN COMPLEXITY

During functional allocation, requirements are assigned to major components or subsystems. System design further partitions the required functionality and data of a software system into small parts that work together to achieve the full mission of the system. Thus, system design complexity can be viewed as having two components: the complexity contained within each part defined by the design and the complexity of the relationships among the parts. During unit design, the procedural structure of each of these parts is defined (or elaborated). Fig. 5–1 shows the relationships among design activities and products.

In the following discussion, we will refer to design parts as modules, in the sense that a module is the smallest independently compilable unit of code [42]. Each design part will eventually be implemented as a software module. In a FORTRAN system, modules correspond to subroutines. Of course, any complete design must include nonmodule parts such as files and COMMON blocks (in FORTRAN). Moreover, partitioning is not the only design process. Nevertheless, the many different design approaches (or methods) achieve the same design result: a high-level architectural design and an integrated set of individual module designs.

5-1-1 Functional Complexity

At the front end of design (functional allocation), complexity measurement merges with cost estimation. The designer's principal concern is to understand the magnitude and nature (complexity) of the requirements. Often, only the number and type of functions are known. Even this may be difficult to determine from a natural-language requirements specification.

The magnitude (or number) of requirements determines the size of the software product that must be built. However, some applications are inherently more difficult (complex) than others. Table 5–1 shows the complexity classification

TABLE 5-1. FUNCTIONAL COMPLEXITY SCALE

Rating	Control Operations	Computational Operations	Device-dependent Operations	Data Management Operations
Very low	Straightline code with a few non-nested SP[a] operators: DOs, CASEs, IFTHENELSEs. Simple predicates	Evaluation of simple expressions: e.g., $A = B + C * (D - E)$	Simple read, write statements with simple formats	Simple arrays in main memory
Low	Straightforward nesting of SP operators. Mostly simple predicates	Evaluation of moderate-level expressions, e.g., $D = SQRT(B**2-4.*A*C)$	No cognizance needed of particular processor or I/O device characteristics. I/O done at GET/PUT level. No cognizance of overlap	Single file subsetting with no data structure changes, no edits, no intermediate files
Nominal	Mostly simple nesting. Some inter-module control. Decision tables	Use of standard math and statistical routines. Basic matrix/vector operations	I/O processing includes device selection, status checking and error processing	Multi-file input and single file output. Simple structural changes, simple edits
High	Highly nested SP operators with many compound predicates. Queue and stack control. Considerable intermodule control.	Basic numerical analysis: multivariate interpolation, ordinary differential equations. Basic truncation, roundoff concerns	Operations at physical I/O level (physical storage address translations; seeks, reads, etc). Optimized I/O overlap	Special purpose subroutines activated by data stream contents. Complex data restructuring at record level
Very high	Reentrant and recursive coding. Fixed-priority interrupt handling	Difficult but structured N.A.: near-singular matrix equations, partial differential equations	Routines for interrupt diagnosis, servicing, masking. Communication line handling	A generalized, parameter-driven file structuring routine. File building, command processing, search optimization
Extra high	Multiple resource scheduling with dynamically changing priorities. Microcode-level control	Difficult and unstructured N.A.: highly accurate analysis of noisy, stochastic data	Device timing-dependent coding, micro-programmed operations	Highly coupled, dynamic relational structures. Natural language data management

[a] SP = structured programming

(Reprinted from B. W. Boehm, *Software Engineering Economics,* Prentice-Hall, 1981, by permission.)

scheme developed by Boehm [10] for software cost estimation. The designer has little influence on most of the factors described in this figure.

Thus, although functional allocation manipulates the functional complexity of a software system, it is driven primarily by the nature of the problem to be solved. No matter how much we wish we could control functional complexity, for the most part that control is beyond our reach. We must concentrate, then, on minimizing the subsequent complexities, shown in the center diagonal of Fig. 5–1, beginning with the system design activity.

5-1-2 System Design Complexity

The minimum possible (or inherent) complexity of a software design is established by its functionality (the nature and amount of work performed within the system). However, in a large system, it is necessary to divide the large problem into smaller units rather than implement it in one piece. This decomposition, although necessary to the problem-solving process, introduces new opportunities for complexity. Mc-Clure [35], for example, distinguishes between the complexity of connections between modules (intermodule complexity) and the internal structure of each module (intramodule complexity). How the work is divided up into modules during system design heavily affects complexity and produceability.

Functional decomposition (the basis of structured design [42]) is one common approach to system design. It results in a hierarchical network of units (or modules). For any module, workload consists of input and output items to be processed (see Fig. 5–2; note that the I/O items form the "data coupling" for the module). At

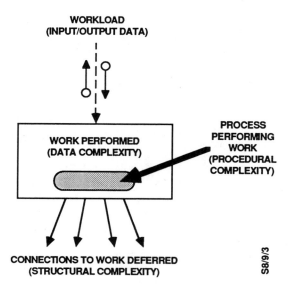

Figure 5–2. Decomposition model of system design

each level of decomposition, the designer must decide whether to implement the indicated functionality (perform the work) in the current module or defer some of it to a lower level by invoking one or more other modules (control coupling). Similar decisions also must be made when following other design approaches (e.g., object-oriented [51]).

Deferring functionality decreases the local data (intramodule) complexity but also increases the structural (intermodule) complexity. This results in a law of "incomplete conservation of complexity"; you can push complexity around but you can't get rid of it entirely. Moreover, the actual complexity of a poorly partitioned design may be much greater than the minimun possible complexity corresponding to its functionality.

System Complexity Measure. As shown in Fig. 5–2, work performed (within modules) as well as the connections among the work parts (modules) are the constituents of system complexity. Effective design minimizes work as well as connections. This argument leads to the following formulation for the system complexity of a software design:

$$Ct = St + Dt \qquad\qquad (5-1)$$

where

$$Ct = \text{system complexity}$$
$$St = \text{structural (intermodule) complexity}$$
$$Dt = \text{data (intramodule) complexity}$$

That is, the complexity (Ct) of a system design can be defined as the sum of intermodule plus intramodule complexity. In this simple model, all complexity resides in one or the other of these two components. Hence, they are additive. These complexity components approximate the structured design concepts of module coupling and cohesion defined by Stephens et al. [42].

Note that for the moment we define intramodule complexity to be data complexity. Later we will also discuss intramodule procedural complexity. We defer the latter discussion because in the early stages of system design the nature of the data often precedes and determines the procedural makeup of the module. The distinction between data and procedural complexity parallels the distinction between the specification and the body, respectively, of an Ada* package.

Relative System Complexity. It may be useful to know the overall complexity of a system, but for comparison purposes, it is often more useful to know its relative complexity. Dividing overall complexity by the number of modules defined in the design gives us a normalized, or relative, complexity:

---

*Ada is a registered trademark of the Ada Joint Program Office.

$$C = Ct/n = St/n + Dt/n \qquad (5\text{--}2)$$

where

$$
\begin{aligned}
C &= \text{relative system complexity} \\
Ct &= \text{system complexity (overall)} \\
St &= \text{structural complexity} \\
Dt &= \text{data complexity} \\
n &= \text{number of modules in system}
\end{aligned}
$$

Although individual modules may vary greatly in size in terms of lines of source code, as used here, the module is the unit of design. Hence it is the appropriate normalization factor. All further references to system complexity in what follows will mean relative system complexity as defined here.

The next sections explain measures for both of the system complexity components listed in Eq. (5-2). The measures incorporate counts of the design characteristics identified in the model of Fig. 5-2. These measures correspond to four key "primitive design metrics" defined by DeMarco [11]: calls, variables, modules, and decisions.

5-1-2-1 Structural complexity.

Structural complexity emerges from the relationships among the modules of a system. The most basic relationship is that a module may call or be called by another module. The structurally simplest system consists of a single module with no calls. For more complex systems, structural complexity is the sum of the contributions of these calls. We will measure the complexity contribution of these calls by counting occurrences of fanin and fanout. Fanin is the count of calls to a given module. Fanout is the count of calls from a given module. (For a further analysis of the contribution of fanin and fanout to complexity, see Henry and Kafura [37] and Belady and Evangelisti [36].)

In the SEL data analyzed, multiple fanin (the calling of a module from several places) was generally confined to modules that performed simple mathematical functions reused throughout the system. Consequently, high fanin did not prove to be an important complexity indicator. On the other hand, fanout proved to be more important, as indicated in Sec. 4-3. For that reason, we will use fanout as our measure of structural complexity here. (Counting only fanout also ensures that each connection is counted exactly once.)

It is important to note that it is not just total fanout, but also the distribution of fanout within a system, that affects complexity. The interconnection matrix representation of partitioning used by Belady and Evangelisti [36] suggests that complexity increases as the square of connections (fanout). All descendants of a given module are connected to each other by their common parent. Thus, there are fanout-squared possible connections among the decomposed work parts to concern the software developer.

For a fixed total fanout, then, a system in which invocations are concentrated in a few modules is more complex than one in which invocations are more evenly distributed.

These considerations lead to the following formulation for structural complexity:

$$S = \frac{\Sigma f^2 (i)}{n} \qquad (5\text{-}3)$$

where

$$
\begin{aligned}
S &= \text{structural (intermodule) complexity} \\
f(i) &= \text{fanout of module ``}i\text{''} \\
n &= \text{number of modules in system}
\end{aligned}
$$

Note that we can think of this as the average squared deviation of actual fanout from the simplest structure (zero fanout).

Many similarly constructed measures have been developed. Henry and Kafura's term "(fanin × fanout)^2" [37] reduces to fanout-squared when fanin is assumed equal to one (the nominal case). Belady and Evangelisti's measure of complexity [36] is a function of the number of nodes (modules) and edges (fanout) in a system or cluster (partition). Benyon-Tinker [52] combined similar measures with hierarchical level in his complexity model.

The fanout count defined here does not include calls to system or standard utility routines, but does include calls to modules reused from other application programs. This is because, in order to reuse a module, the designer must examine it to establish its reusability in the given context, as opposed to standard utilities whose internals need not be understood by developers.

5-1-2-2 Data complexity.   The internal complexity of a module is a function of the amount of work it must perform. The workload consists of data items that are input to or output from higher or parallel modules. This definition is consistent with Halstead's concept [20] of the minimal representation of a program as a function (single operator) with an associated set of I/O variables (operands). (This workload measure parallels the idea of "data bindings" as used by Hutchens and Basili [53].)

To the extent that functionality (work) is deferred to lower levels, the internal complexity of a module is reduced. From that we can see that the data complexity of a module is directly dependent on its own I/O complexity and inversely dependent on the I/O complexity it defers to a lower level:

$$D(i) = \frac{V(i)}{f(i) + 1}$$

where

$$
\begin{aligned}
D(i) &= \text{data complexity of module } i \\
V(i) &= \text{I/O variables in module } i \\
f(i) &= \text{fanout of module } i
\end{aligned}
$$

The +1 term represents each module's own share of the fanned-out workload. (Incidentally, it prevents the divide-by-zero condition from arising when a module has no fanout.)

Averaging the internal complexities of a system's component modules should produce its local data complexity. Most guidelines for decomposition suggest decomposing into units of equal functionality. Assuming for simplicity that the workload of a module is evenly divided among itself and subordinate modules leads to the following formulation of local data complexity:

$$D = \frac{\Sigma \{v(i)/[f(i) + 1]\}}{n} \qquad (5\text{--}4)$$

where

$$
\begin{aligned}
D &= \text{data (intramodule) complexity} \\
v(i) &= \text{I/O variables in module } i \\
f(i) &= \text{fanout of module } i \\
n &= \text{number of new modules in system}
\end{aligned}
$$

Ideally, we would consider the fact that different variables have different effects on a system. However, at system design time the effect of each variable may not yet be defined. Because of that, we will treat the data complexity of a module only as the *number* of data items it is expected to process. (Note again that, in a system with reused modules, only newly developed modules enter into this computation.)

What do we mean here by I/O variables? We include distinct arguments in a calling sequence (an array counts as one variable) as well as referenced COMMON variables. (Section 4-2 showed that the presence of unreferenced COMMON variables does not affect module quality.) Unfortunately, the data available for study did not permit consideration of the role of more complex data structures (records, linked lists, etc.) in design complexity.

5-1-3 Procedural Complexity

Once the function and input/output data of a module have been specified, an algorithm must be developed to perform the function and process the data. Part of the complexity of this algorithm can be attributed to the intrinsic difficulty or complexity of the problem. That is the work required to be done by the module (see Fig. 5-2).

Usually, the designer is unable to hold complexity to this minimum; the nature of the solution adds complexity to that of the problem. Design efficiency (avoidance of excess complexity) depends on the methods, tools, people, and environment as well as the nature of the design problem. Many early studies of software complexity focused on process construction and procedural complexity, so this component is relatively well understood (see Chap. 3).

The most widely accepted measure of procedural complexity for the detailed design of a module is cyclomatic complexity [30], or a simple count of the number of decisions (see Sec. 3-2). Warnier [54] suggested that the decision structure of a module depends largely on the quantity and structure of the data; each data item translates into about one decision.

Figure 5–3 shows that the average data complexity of modules in a system effectively predicts the average number of decisions in those modules. The following equation represents a linear fit to those data:

$$\text{Decisions} = 1.3\,D + 7.7 \tag{5–5}$$

In other words, for each unit of data complexity (see Sec. 5-1-2-2), 1.3 decisions must be made to implement the function, and in addition, the average module includes a base of 7.7 decisions not directly related to the module's data function. Given that the average number of decisions per module (in the sample represented in Fig. 5–3) is 19.4, this means that about 40 percent of decisions result from design inefficiency or special implementation considerations. (These considerations might include reformatting data for local use, error handling, and robustness features, such as a check to prevent the divide-by-zero condition.)

Ultimately, the designed module must be implemented in code. Figure 5–4 shows that data complexity effectively predicts the size of a module in terms of executable statements. For this sample, each increase of one unit of data complexity increases program size by four executable statements. This result is consistent with an earlier study; using related data, Basili et al. [55] showed source lines of code to be highly correlated ($r = 0.79$) with the number of I/O variables (operands).

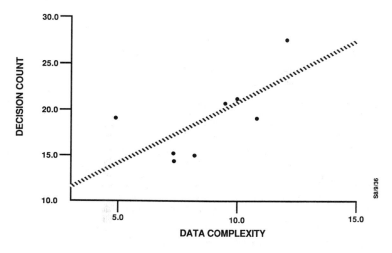

Figure 5–3. Procedural complexity related to data complexity

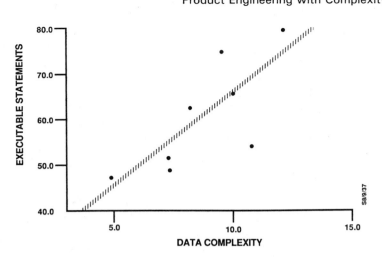

Figure 5–4. Module size related to data complexity

The relationships among data complexity, decisions, and executable statements also depend on the programming language in which the design is eventually implemented. For example, a language like Ada that allows the program to conform more closely to the natural structure of the data should lower the ratio of decisions to data complexity. However, it does not guarantee a lower complexity solution.

5-2 VALIDATING THE COMPLEXITY MODEL

We have shown that design complexity is determined by

- Functional complexity resulting from the problem (that the designer cannot usually control)
- System complexity, including structural complexity and data complexity (that the system designer introduces/controls)
- Procedural complexity (that the unit designer introduces/controls)

We have also shown that the essential measures of complexity are fanout and the number of I/O variables from/in a module.

This forms a very simple and workable model of complexity. The next question to be dealt with is: How good (useful) is this model?

The validity of the model was evaluated in two ways. First, system complexity scores for the eight projects (described in Chap. 2) were compared with a subjective rating of design quality using a nonparametric statistical technique. Then system and procedural complexity scores were compared with objective measures of development error rate, development productivity, and software maintainability using linear regression. Productivity and error rates were computed using the developed source lines of code measure as defined by Basili and Freburger [15] (see Sec. 2-3).

Table 5–2 lists the complexity scores for the eight projects studied. All of these systems were designed and implemented to run with a common interactive graphics interface. It occupies level 1 of every design hierarchy. It is not included in the complexity calculations. Because all were flight dynamics projects, their functional complexities (in terms of application type) were equivalent. Section 6-1 reports results related to magnitude (number of subsystems) under software size estimation.

These eight projects represent lots of data items, as described in Sec. 2-3. Each of nearly 2,000 modules was individually analyzed. The module scores were combined by project to form the points shown on the graphs in this chapter. Dealing with the projects simplifies both the computation and the presentation of the results—imagine these graphs with 2,000 points. However, looking back to Chap. 4 you will see that these results are consistent with the results of the module level studies reported there (which did involve larger samples).

5-2-1 Subjective Quality

Because system design complexity forms a major component of fitness for use, it should show general agreement with a subjective measure of overall design quality. To assess this, the eight projects were subjectively ranked in order from best to worst, in terms of design quality, by a senior manager who participated in the development of all eight projects. Then the four best rated designs were classified as "good" and the other four were classified as "poor." Table 5–3 shows the results of that procedure.

The table also includes the system complexity measure. Note that the four designs subjectively rated as "good" also demonstrated the lowest relative complexity. The expert was not provided with specific criteria for "quality," but later reported that perceived "complexity" played a major role in assigning scores.

Although the correspondence (shown in Table 5–3) between subjective design

TABLE 5–2. COMPLEXITY SCORES FOR EIGHT FLIGHT DYNAMICS SYSTEMS

PROJECT	NUMBER OF SUBSYSTEMS	AVERAGE COMPLEXITY		
		STRUCTURAL	DATA	PROCEDURAL
A	6	24.6	8.2	15.1
B	8	15.8	9.5	21.0
C	14	11.8	12.1	28.0
D	9	18.4	4.9	19.4
E	12	12.6	10.0	21.8
F	15	22.3	7.3	15.2
G	8	18.3	10.8	19.7
H	7	19.2	7.3	14.7

S8/9/8

TABLE 5-3. DESIGN COMPLEXITY AND QUALITY

PROJECT	SYSTEM COMPLEXITY[a]	DESIGN RATING[b]	QUALITY CLASS
A	32.8	5	POOR
B	25.3	2	GOOD
C	23.9	3	GOOD
D	23.3	1	GOOD
E	22.6	4	GOOD
F	29.6	6	POOR
G	29.1	8	POOR
H	26.5	7	POOR

[a] C = S + L AS PREVIOUSLY DEFINED (EQUATIONS 5-2, 5-3, 5-4).
[b] SUBJECTIVE EVALUATION (1 = BEST, 8 = WORST).

rating and objective system complexity is not one for one, viewed as quality classes the data provide persuasive evidence for a relationship. (The probability is less than 0.02, using the Wilcoxon rank sum statistic, that the observed good/poor groupings could occur by chance alone.) Thus, the objective complexity measure appears to capture much of the information that a human observer includes in a subjective evaluation of design quality.

5-2-2 Development Error Rate

Designers and researchers commonly assume that higher complexity increases the propensity for error, that is, errors are more likely to occur in a complex system than in a simple one. However, high complexity does not necessarily mean that an error has occurred. Potier et al. [56] observe that, for a well-designed system, the implementation process consists largely of translating design specifications into a programming language. It usually does not add much complexity to a system.

Weiss and Basili [9] show that the bulk, 74 to 82 percent, of all nonclerical errors reported in three of these SEL projects were design-related, although sometimes at very detailed levels. Very few of these errors were strictly programming errors (see Fig. 1-7). Of course, many detailed design and implementation errors (not counted here) are detected during unit design inspections, code reading, and unit testing.

Figure 5-5 illustrates the relationship between system complexity and error rate. It shows that system complexity effectively predicts the total error rate for development projects. The correlation coefficient of 0.83 was significant at the 0.02 level. Complexity (as measured here) accounts for fully 69 percent of the variation in error rate. The following equation captures the relationship:

$$\text{Error rate} = 0.4 \text{ complexity} - 5.2 \tag{5-6}$$

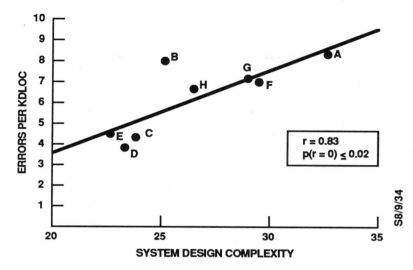

Figure 5-5. Error rate increases with system design complexity

Each increase of one unit of complexity increases the error rate by 0.4 (errors per 1,000 lines). None of the projects studied approached the minimum complexity of about five that corresponds to an error rate of zero.

As seen in Fig. 5-5, all but one of the points lie very close to the regression line. In that one case, project B, the implementation team consisted of an unusually large proportion of junior personnel (although its design team was comparable to those of the other projects). Consequently, it seems reasonable to find a higher error rate than would be indicated by system design complexity alone.

Thus, both personnel experience and complexity drive the error rate. In small systems where the designer is the programmer, design complexity is less important to error rate; experience is the major factor.

5-2-3 Development Productivity

Functional complexity and magnitude set the basic cost of a system (see Secs. 5-1-1 and 6-1). However, the productivity achieved during development affects the final cost. Figure 5-6 illustrates the relationship between system design complexity and productivity. Although suggestive, the observed trend in these data is not statistically significant. Nor did the data support the existence of a relationship between development productivity and procedural complexity. However, other researchers (e.g., Gaffney [57]) have reported finding higher implementation productivity associated with lower procedural complexity (number of decisions).

In many environments, the development process affects productivity more than the complexity of the design. A good design will result in less rework (fewer errors), but the process by which the design is implemented and errors are rectified

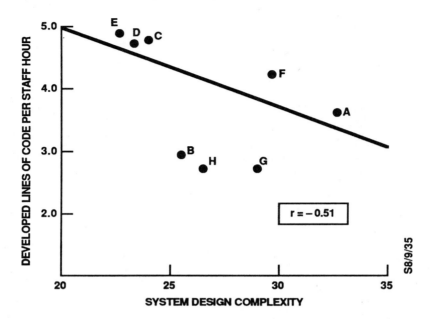

Figure 5-6. Productivity not tightly linked to system design complexity

obscures this effect. Moreover, an inefficient process may produce unnecessary complexity, even though the excess complexity costs as much to implement as the necessary (essential) complexity (see Sec. 5-3-4).

Figure 5–7 plots the relationship between computer use (a process measure) and productivity in the SEL environment. Extensive computer use (in terms of computer hours per line of code) tends to coincide with low developer productivity. (Similar results from SEL have been reported in terms of terminals per programmer [58]). On the surface this appears to conflict with conventional wisdom about the benefits of ample computer support.

Understanding this relationship requires a look at the time order of events to distinguish cause from effect. Figure 5–8 shows the typical pattern for computer use in the SEL environment. Computer support was provided to these projects primarily during detailed (unit) design, coding, and testing (the last half of the life cycle). Software tools include basic items like editors, compilers, and library utilities.

Note that most computer use occurs during testing (after 60 to 80 percent of the effort has been expended). Thus, high computer use indicates the presence of development problems that result in an "integration and testing crunch." These problems usually manifest themselves as software errors. Because testing and debugging are computer-intensive activities, these results suggest that complexity indirectly affects productivity by increasing the likelihood of error, thus resulting in more computer use while implementing corrections.

High computer use may also signify intentional reliance on the computer (com-

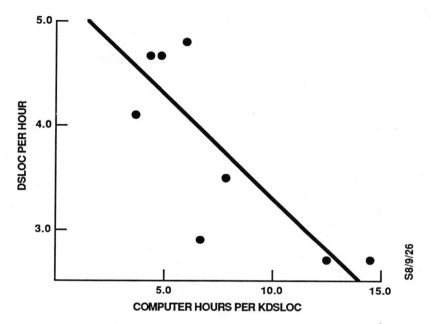

Figure 5-7. High productivity associated with low computer use

piling and testing) to detect errors instead of desk checking. High computer use appears to be a symptom that helps to diagnose the nature of development problems rather than a direct cause of low productivity. Paradoxically, part of the solution may be to provide more computer support to up-front design activities in the form of workstations and software tools.

Many other factors—in particular, programmer experience and ability—also affect productivity. In this organization, the design team forms the nucleus of the implementation and test teams. Additional personnel join as needed. Thus, the complexity measure provides an early indication of the performance of the development team as well as of the quality of the design. A good design team is likely to be a good implementation and testing team, although total productivity may be difficult to predict from system design complexity alone.

5-2-4 Software Maintainability

A good design should facilitate software maintenance, another important component of fitness for use. The unit of maintenance is the module. The maintainer usually works in a module-by-module manner. Maintainability means that changes tend to be confined to localized areas of the system (modules) and are easy to make.

Figure 5-9 shows that procedural complexity (data complexity plus excess complexity) predicts both the proportion of changes that were easy to implement ($r = -0.77$) and the proportion of changes that affected only one module ($r =$

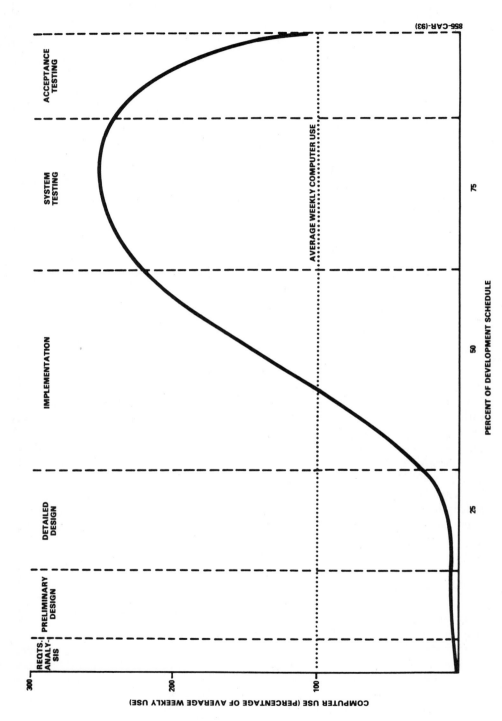

Figure 5–8. Computer use over time for a typical project

58

−0.82). Although both these trends were significant, the correlation between them ($r = 0.61$) was not. That is, localization of change and effort to change are (at least partially) independent aspects of maintainability related to procedural complexity.

Increased procedural complexity means that a change is more likely to propagate to another module, even though the modules are larger. Intuition may suggest that larger modules are more likely to be self-contained, but the data argue against that. Because structured programming affects procedural complexity most strongly (see Sec. 5-3-4), its benefits are most likely to show up during maintenance, as claimed by early advocates. These results support that contention.

5-3 ACHIEVING A LOW COMPLEXITY DESIGN

In Sec. 5-1 we defined a simple and workable model of design complexity. In Sec. 5-2 we validated that model against

- Subjective expert opinions
- Error rate data

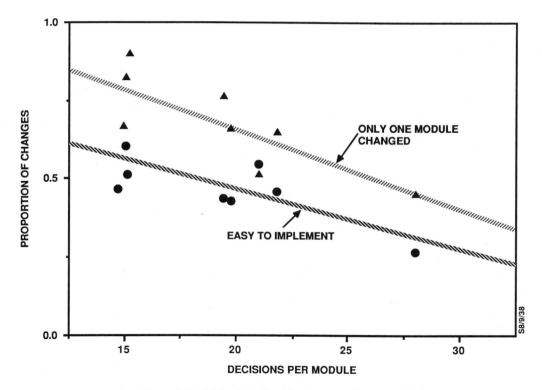

Figure 5–9. Maintainability related to procedural complexity

- Productivity data
- Maintainability data.

It is now time to turn our attention to the use of that model in doing and evaluating software design.

A natural goal for design is low complexity. This model provides measures, sometimes called figures of merit, that allow us to know when we have achieved that low complexity. Figures of merit do that by helping to resolve issues like selecting the best "central transform" when converting a structured analysis into a structured design and deciding when to stop decomposing a design.

Of course, because functional complexity derives from the nature of the problem (see Chap. 1), there is a lower limit to how much complexity can be reduced while still performing the required work. The developer cannot control functional complexity. Consideration of the model of Fig. 5–2 and the corresponding complexity equations earlier in this chapter suggests four basic strategies for minimizing design complexity: optimizing module complexity (Sec. 5-3-1), minimizing data variables (Sec. 5-3-2), minimizing connections (Sec. 5-3-3), and increasing design efficiency (Sec. 5-3-4).

Minimizing structural complexity requires minimizing the fanout from each module. Because our use of fanout involves its square, total fanout for a system is minimized if fanout is balanced across the system (e.g., 2 squared + 2 squared < 1 squared + 3 squared). On the other hand, data complexity can be minimized by minimizing the number of variables or maximizing fanout. Because the latter strategy affects structural complexity negatively, the designer must employ an optimization procedure. (Procedural complexity is, of course, minimized also by minimizing the number of data variables.) Thus, the number of goals to be satisfied is small, but the way of achieving them requires some knowledge and judgment.

The following sections explain the four basic strategies for complexity optimization in detail. The successful designer applies all of them to some extent.

5-3-1 Optimize Module Complexity

System complexity can be reduced by optimizing the complexity between and within its modules. The key to those complexity factors are fanout and the count of I/O variables.

Because fanout contributes both positively and negatively to complexity, let us analyze how we might minimize that contribution. From Eqs. (5–3) and (5–4), we see that, for any individual module, complexity is computed as

$$c = f^2 + v/(f + 1) \qquad (5-7)$$

where

$$c = \text{contribution of given module to total complexity}$$
$$f = \text{fanout of the module}$$
$$v = \text{I/O variables used by the module}$$

We would like to solve that equation for f, fanout. But the equation does not lend itself to a simple algebraic solution. Instead, then, because our goal here is to obtain the fanout value that causes minimum complexity, we will take the partial derivative of complexity with respect to fanout:

$$\partial c/\partial f = 2f - v/(f + 1)^2$$

We then set that derivative to zero:

$$0 = 2f - v/(f + 1)^2$$

and express v as a function of f:

$$v = 2f(f + 1)^2 \tag{5-8}$$

Even here, clarifying the relationship between f and v is a complex algebraic problem. Instead, let us plot this equation for some realistic, representative values of f to see if that visibility helps us.

Figure 5-10 shows a plot of Eq. (5-8) as a step function (to reflect the discrete natures of v and f). It identifies the fanout that minimizes complexity for possible counts of I/O variables. For example, in the range from about 100 to 200 I/O variables, complexity is minimized with a fanout of three. For fewer I/O variables, a

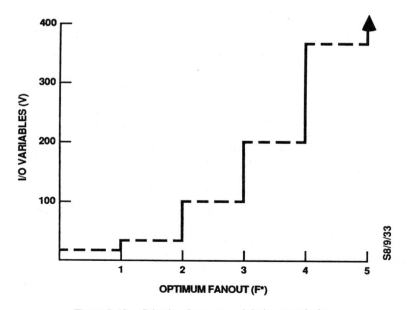

Figure 5-10. Selecting fanout to minimize complexity

fanout of two or less is more appropriate. Because very few modules include as many as 200 I/O variables, the plot indicates that the commonly accepted range of values for fanout (up to 7 ± 2) is much too large. Instead, fanouts of zero, one, or two appear to represent the optimum.

Curtis [19] suggests that the popularity of this 7 ± 2 bound derives from a misunderstanding of certain psychological studies (i.e., [59]). This agrees with the results of Sec. 4-3. Furthermore, Constantine, in [42], observes that most programs can be decomposed effectively into a common structure of three parts: input, process, and output. Larger fanouts may indicate that the decomposition is too rapid. These results also suggest that a fanout of one is a reasonable value for modules with few I/O variables. (Note that these conclusions are contrary to most guidelines for system decomposition; they suggest that module hierarchies should be deep and well balanced rather than flat and/or skewed.)

Figure 5–10 also indicates that no further decomposition is needed for modules containing eight (or fewer) data items. The 7 ± 2 rule [59] appears to apply at this level rather than at the level of module calls. Following Eq. (5–5), a module with eight data items (and fanout of zero) can be expected to have about 12 decisions, if "excess" procedural complexity is avoided. This isn't too far from McCabe's recommended maximum (see Sec. 3-2).

5-3-2 Minimize Data Variables

In addition to selecting an appropriate fanout, design complexity can also be minimized by reducing the number of data variables. One obvious way to do this is to reduce variable repetition or redundancy, that is, by not including variables where they are not needed. Repetition occurs whenever a data item appears in more than one module as a calling sequence argument or referenced common variable, particularly where a data item is passed down through multiple levels in a calling hierarchy. Internal uses (including CALLS to other modules) do not count as repetition.

In general, minimizing data complexity will produce smaller modules (in terms of executable statements), but also may increase structural complexity disproportionately. This results from the law of incomplete conservation of complexity (see Sec. 5-1-2). Rigorous application of the principle of information hiding [43] should reduce variable repetition and, hence, data complexity without necessarily increasing fanout and structural complexity.

Figure 5–11 shows two design segments of equal structural complexity; the number and distribution of fanouts are identical. Each data couple represents a repetition of the variable X. Figure 5–11a traces this variable through a design following strict top-down decomposition rules. X appears in the higher level modules (A, B, D) as well as the lower level modules (C, E).

Figure 5–11b shows an alternative design with a horizontal transfer of data that bypasses the higher level modules (for the case in which modules A, B, and D do not actually use X. The local complexity of the intermediate modules (B, D)

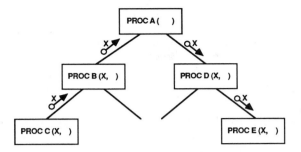

(a) STRICT TOP-DOWN STRUCTURED DESIGN

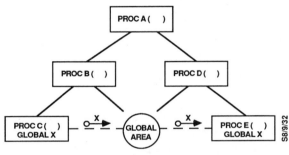

(b) LOWER COMPLEXITY WITH LATERAL TRANSFER

Figure 5-11. Reducing variable repetition to minimize complexity

in the strict top-down configuration (Fig. 5–11a) exceeds their counterparts in the alternative design (Fig. 5–11b) because their counts of I/O variables are larger.

Parameter transfer between hierarchically adjacent modules (e.g., from B to A) produces a lower complexity than transfer via a global area when that is as far as the data item goes. For a triplet connection (e.g., from B to A to D), the two approaches have the same complexity (X counts twice in each). Because this model emphasizes the number of data couples rather than the nature of the coupling mechanism, it penalizes "tramp data" (data passed through but not referenced by a module).

Rotenstreich and Howden [60] argue that both horizontal and vertical data flow are essential to good design. Appropriate use of horizontal transfers prevents data flows from violating levels of abstraction. COMMON blocks provide the only mechanism for horizontal data transfers in FORTRAN. Figure 5–11 shows that horizontal data flows can reduce the magnitude of the data complexity measure in some situations.

Of course, a less complex design might also be produced by partitioning the work differently and restructuring this design. For example, PROC C could be invoked directly by PROC E to obtain X (if the nature of the problem permitted). This simpler structure would also be reflected in lower values of the complexity measures defined by this model. (PROCs B and C would each have fanout of one instead of PROC B having fanout of two. Thus, structural complexity diminishes.)

Note that once again we have arrived at a conclusion contrary to some usual guidelines. Minimizing complexity through data variable usage may involve such things as using common data rather than parameter passing, especially to avoid tramp data, and rearranging module call hierarchies to minimize data passing. Traditionally, computer science has argued strongly *against* the use of common data.

5-3-3 Minimize Connections

We have seen that fanout and the number of I/O variables are critical to the complexity of a software design. Distributing fanout evenly across the modules in a design (except for terminal nodes) minimizes structural complexity, and for any module, the fanout for minimum complexity depends on the number of I/O variables present.

Another indicator of complexity is the number of modules present at any hierarchical level in the design. The number of modules at any level, of course, corresponds to the fanout count at the preceding level.

On well-conceived projects, we will show here, there is a well-defined and recognizable relationship among these three measures. Table 5–4 shows the distribution of these measures by hierarchical level for one project. The data are then represented graphically, as shown in Fig. 5–12, by plotting the cumulative percentage of these quantities obtained at each level. The representation of Fig. 5–12 is termed a ''profile.''

Notice two things about Fig. 5–12. All three variables—fanout, I/O variables, and modules—track quite well with one another. Furthermore, the curve has a distinct S shape: The growth of the three variables starts out slowly, then increases

TABLE 5–4. DETAILED DESIGN STRUCTURE FOR PROJECT E

HIERARCHICAL LEVEL	NUMBER OF MODULES	MODULE AVERAGE		
		EXECUTABLE STATEMENTS	FANOUT	INPUT/OUTPUT VARIABLES
2	2	91	6.5	45
3	4	37	4.8	9
4	19	59	5.6	29
5	93	67	2.2	26
6	62	59	2.0	24
7	54	59	1.8	20
8	33	37	1.4	14
9	7	19	0.7	8
$\geq$10	2	8	0.0	5
UTILITY	51	90	2.4	21

S8/9/31

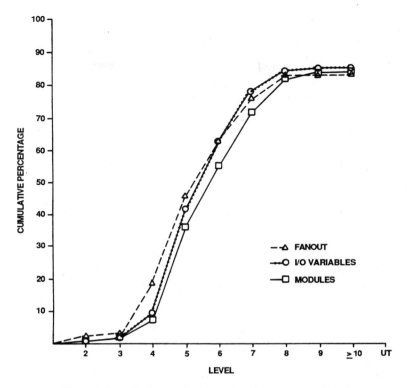

Figure 5-12. Design profile of project E (lowest complexity)

rapidly, and finally tails off at the end. The reason for these phenomena is that the conditions that minimize structural complexity result in an even distribution of fanout. This produces an increasing growth rate in the cumulative percentage of total fanout in the initial levels of the design, followed by a gradual decrease in growth rate as hierarchical module subtrees terminate.

Figure 5-12 illustrates project E, the design with the lowest relative complexity. As we have discussed, it shows three closely fitted S-shaped curves. Compare the curves with those in Fig. 5-13.

Figure 5-13 illustrates project A, the design with the highest relative complexity. It shows three separate and irregular lines, with no S shape. Profiles of the other six projects fall in between these two extremes. The irregularity of Fig. 5-13 arises because of unevenly distributed fanout. This causes an irregular plot of cumulative fanout.

Note: In Figs. 5-12 and 5-13, the design structure (or profile) is simplified by combining all utility modules, regardless of where invoked, into a single deepest level of the design. That point is not plotted. (''Utility'' refers to new or reused modules that are invoked from more than one point within a design, but not system

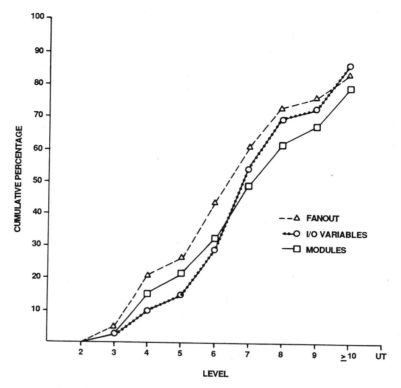

Figure 5-13.   Design profile of project A (highest complexity)

or standard utilities.) Hierarchical levels greater than or equal to ten are also combined into a single level to facilitate plotting.

In order to determine if a design is on track for minimum complexity, then, one can plot these three variables in the indicated way and see if the plots track and form the desired S curve. If they do not, then the solution is to examine the fanout distribution and adjust it. This can be accomplished both by balancing the fanout at a given level and by adjusting the levels of hierarchy (perhaps by interjecting a new level between two current levels to help balance the calls, as discussed by Kafura and Henry [61]). The result of these adjustments is to minimize the number of connections in the design. Using this approach, then, early detection of design complexity problems is possible, and the necessary repair work can be performed before the design is carried out too deeply.

Interestingly, some data are available on what happens as each of projects E and A move on into detail design and implementation in an environment where work is largely ordered top-down.

In Fig. 5-14, we see a resource utilization profile for each of these two projects. The figure plots hours of effort charged to each of the projects over time. The

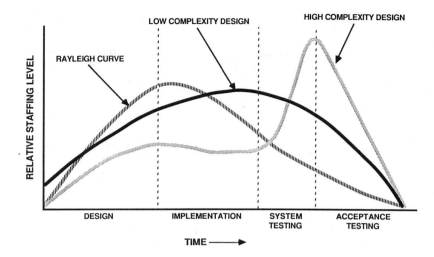

1 ADAPTED FROM F. E. McGARRY, "MEASURING SOFTWARE DEVELOPMENT TECHNOLOGY," PROCEEDINGS: SEVENTH ANNUAL SOFTWARE ENGINEERING WORKSHOP, NASA/GSFC, DECEMBER 1982

0110S(1)-10

Figure 5–14. Complexity affects development profile

low complexity design allows gradual tapering off of activity as the project proceeds, much like a standard Rayleigh curve, whereas the high complexity design leads to an "integration crunch" as significant design decisions are made deep in the design structure, where they are implemented late in the development process. Clearly, this kind of last-minute crunch is harmful to project costs and schedules, product quality, and the morale of the people associated with the project.

5-3-4 Increase Design Efficiency

Recall that procedural complexity can be minimized by minimizing the number of decisions in the design. Because each decision defined must be coded, tested, and maintained, designing close to some lower bound of decisions is important for cost and maintainability.

Most modern programming practices contribute to the capability to produce designs close to such a lower bound. To the extent that the product is carefully planned and conceived, it will exhibit more simplicity. Table 5–5 defines a fairly representative set of such modern programming practices (MPPs). Each of these MPPs adds order and structure to the software development process.

McCabe [30] and McClure [35] argue, for example, that well-structured programs exhibit lower complexity than unstructured ones. Poor methods and inexperi-

TABLE 5-5.   MODERN PROGRAMMING PRACTICES (AS DEFINED BY BOEHM [10])

PRACTICE	DEFINITION
TOP-DOWN REQUIREMENTS ANALYSIS AND DESIGN	DEVELOPMENT OF SOFTWARE REQUIREMENTS AND DESIGN AS A SEQUENCE OF HIERARCHICAL ELABORATIONS OF THE USERS' INFORMATION PROCESSING NEEDS AND OBJECTIVES
STRUCTURED DESIGN NOTATION	USE OF A MODULAR, HIERARCHICAL DESIGN NOTATION (PROGRAM DESIGN LANGUAGE, STRUCTURE CHARTS, HIPO) CONSISTENT WITH THE STRUCTURED CODE CONSTRUCTS (SEE BELOW)
TOP-DOWN INCREMENTAL DEVELOPMENT	DETAILED DESIGN, CODE, AND INTEGRATION PERFORMED AS A SEQUENCE OF HIERARCHICAL ELABORATIONS OF THE SOFTWARE STRUCTURE
DESIGN AND CODE WALKTHROUGHS OR INSPECTIONS	PREPLANNED PEER REVIEWS OF THE DETAILED DESIGN AND OF THE CODE OF EACH SOFTWARE UNIT
STRUCTURED CODE	USE OF MODULAR, HIERARCHICAL CONTROL STRUCTURES BASED ON A SMALL NUMBER OF ELEMENTARY CONTROL STRUCTURES, EACH HAVING ONLY ONE FLOW OF CONTROL IN AND OUT
PROGRAM LIBRARIAN	PROJECT PARTICIPANT RESPONSIBLE FOR OPERATING AN ORGANIZED REPOSITORY AND CONTROL SYSTEM FOR SOFTWARE COMPONENTS

0168S(4)-17

ence produce inordinately complex modules. Figure 5–15 shows the eight SEL projects classified with respect to the MPPs of Table 5–5. Those projects with higher MPP use tended to produce modules with lower "excess" complexity (as defined in Sec. 5-1-3). The exception, project B, employed a less experienced programming team than did the other projects.

Unnecessary complexity means unnecessary software. In this unnecessary software will be excess decisions, adding (as we have seen) to the procedural complexity of the result. This increased complexity then results in a higher cost to deliver the required functionality.

Note: The *productivity* of implementing unnecessary software may be the same as or higher than that of the necessary software. Productivity measures like lines of code per hour, then, can give only a crude indication of process efficiency. They may, in fact, give entirely misleading information, as they cannot distinguish between efficient production of necessary code and efficient production of unnecessary code.

Identifying and measuring inefficiency is the first step toward correcting it. Unit design reviews help to stabilize the design process and keep excess complexity down (see Sec. 7-1). Over the long term, however, increasing design efficiency requires improved training, tools, and methods (see Sec. 8-2).

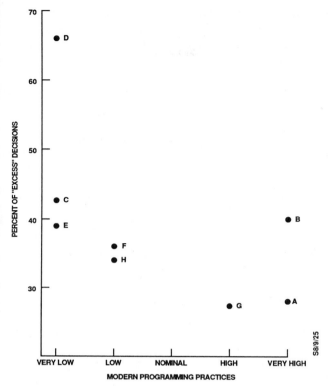

Figure 5-15. MPP use reduces "excess" complexity

Thus, the design process chosen can significantly contribute to the efficiency of the resulting design. In addition to the other approaches suggested in this chapter, well-chosen modern programming practices can help produce designs and code that are measurably better than those produced without them.

5-4 SUMMARY

This chapter has explored some basic relationships between software design complexity and the factors that contribute to that complexity. We have seen that complexity consists of

- Functional complexity
- System complexity, defined by structural complexity and data complexity
- Procedural complexity

Furthermore, we have seen that the key measures of complexity, and thus the points at which designers can effect the most change in design complexity, are fanout and the number of I/O data variables.

Identification of these factors, and establishing expressions for evaluating them, resulted in a simple but workable model of complexity. Empirical validation of that model was then undertaken, and in most cases that exploration was satisfactory. Thus, the model is presented here with some confidence that it will be helpful in designing software and in evaluating software designs.

Toward that end, specific approaches to using the model were examined. Recommended were

- Optimizing module complexity (fanout should be held to three or less)
- Minimizing data variables (using common data and rearranging module call structures can minimize data complexity)
- Minimizing connections (fanout, the number of I/O variables, and the count of the number of modules should conform to similar, S-shaped curves)
- Increasing design efficiency (modern programming practices should be used)

Some of these recommendations run counter to traditional thinking in both the theoretical and pragmatic worlds of computing, while others are solidly in the mainstream. That should not be too surprising, given the young age of the professions of computer science researcher and software engineer.

The bottom line of Chap. 5 is that the application of the model should help the designer to optimize a software design in terms of produceability while still satisfying customer requirements.

6

Software Project Estimation

Whereas Part II explained how software engineers use complexity measures to guide design decisions, Part III describes how complexity and other measures help managers perform their basic functions of planning and controlling a software project. The development manager needs objective criteria for project estimation (Chap. 6), quality control (Chap. 7), and process improvement (Chap. 8). Managers often rely on project control and product assurance experts to assist in these functions.

A software project begins with the production of a development plan that identifies the work to be performed, budget, and schedule. Effective project planning depends on accurate cost estimation. Because of its immense practical importance, this area of measurement application has received a lot of successful attention—in spite of the fact that cost estimation occurs at a much earlier stage of the life cycle for software than for manufactured products. Usually manufacturers and builders estimate costs from a complete design rather than just requirements.

Typically, software project estimation proceeds in four steps:

1. Estimate the size of software to be developed.
2. Compute the cost to develop that software.

3. Develop a schedule for building the software.
4. Monitor performance and adjust estimates periodically.

Although the following sections discuss these steps in some detail, this is not meant to be a text on software cost estimation (for that, see Boehm [10]). This discussion only makes some observations that point to collecting the right data for project estimation, regardless of the particular model or method of estimation used.

6-1 ESTIMATE SOFTWARE SIZE

Verner and Tate [63] argue that software sizing is the weak link in the software cost estimation chain. Most models expect an estimate of lines of code or delivered source instructions as input. Figure 6–1a shows that, within a specific application type, a simple count of the number of subsystems (major functions) accurately predicts the delivered size of the software system. (The correlation coefficient of 0.90 is significant at the 0.01 level.) On the other hand, Fig. 6–1b indicates that this measure doesn't do as well (by itself) at predicting development cost. (Although a

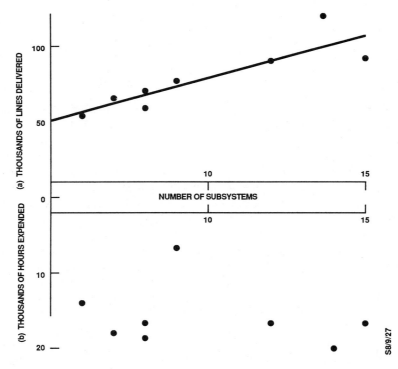

Figure 6–1. Using subsystems to predict system size and cost

linear fit is possible, it tends to show that cost is constant no matter how many subsystems there are.) This inadequacy is probably due to the fact that so many other cost factors intervene. For example, software reuse varies among these projects from 11 to 84 percent. These other factors need to be considered after the initial size estimate has been made.

Others have used counts of subsystems and data sets to predict the size (and cost) of business information systems. Albrecht's function points approach [64] provides a more sophisticated technique for counting functions and interfaces for data processing systems. Estimators usually convert function points directly to a cost estimate but could instead produce a size estimate for input to productivity models [63].

Whatever the method chosen for size estimation, it is important that the organization intending to make the estimates collect historic data useful for that method. For example, if the function point method is chosen, then the organization should collect data by application domain on the number of function points in particular projects, the resultant size estimates, the adjustments made to the estimates as milestones are passed, and finally, the actual versus estimated size. These data can then be used to refine future estimates, and in particular to refine the organization-specific constants appearing in some of the equations to be discussed in the sections of this book to come.

6-2 COMPUTE SOFTWARE COST

Basically, software cost is computed by multiplying the units of software size by appropriate productivity factors. Most cost equations take the form

$$E = p\,L^c$$

where

E = effort in staff months
p = productivity adjustment
L = size in lines of code
$c > 1$, a constant

The productivity adjustment (p) may be a single factor or a composite of factors, as in COCOMO [10]. Making the exponential constant (c) slightly greater than one causes overall productivity to decline with increasing project size. However, for projects in the same size range, this equation reduces to just productivity times size; assume c equal to one and adjust p accordingly.

The principal factors in determining productivity are, in rough order of importance, personnel ability, application complexity, software reuse, and technology applied. Boehm [10] deals with these factors (and more) in great detail. However, he also points out that COCOMO [10] and all such models need to be calibrated with data from the user's environment. Often, rules of thumb based on local data do better than cost models. Users frequently misunderstand the models, but usually do know what their own data mean (how staff months, lines of code, application types, etc., are defined). See Appendix C for examples of such rules of thumb.

As previously mentioned, productivity is most influenced by the people chosen to do the job. After people, the type of work performed influences productivity the most. For example, COCOMO calls for adjusting the DSI (size) estimate to account for reuse before applying any productivity factors. Figure 6–2 shows how productivity (in terms of DSIs per staff day) varies with programming task. Reusing existing software in a new system is three times as productive as developing new code. On the other hand, fixing errors in existing software proceeds at only one-fourth the base productivity rate. Part of this variation in productivity results from the fact that DSIs are not a good measure of work for all programming tasks (see [84] for a discussion).

6-3 DEVELOP SCHEDULE

The next step after defining the work and estimating its cost is to develop a schedule for product activities. The optimum time to completion for a project is often defined with an equation of the form

$$T = a \, E^b$$

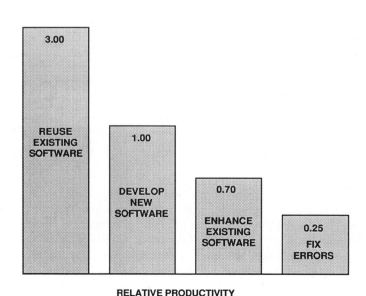

RELATIVE PRODUCTIVITY

Figure 6–2.   Productivity for different software tasks

where

$$T = \text{time to completion in months}$$
$$a = \text{about 2.5, a constant}$$
$$b = \text{about 0.4, a constant}$$

Boehm [10] offers a different set of constants for each of three types of software projects (embedded, semidetached, and organic). However, for those organizations working within a particular application domain and environment, one set of constants will suffice—but it should be determined from an analysis of local data.

Most software estimation experts recommend the use of a Rayleigh curve, like that shown in Fig. 6–3, to distribute effort across the determined time period. Individual development activities (i.e., design, code, test) can be modeled as individual Rayleigh curves that sum to the total project staffing level. Often, however, the schedule is constrained by customer requirements and staffing limitations. The resultant staffing profile may be flat. Figure 6–3 shows how a Rayleigh curve may be modified so that personnel are not being hired or fired every month.

Experts agree that reducing a schedule to less than 75 percent of the optimum time (T) is nearly impossible. Thus, although the Rayleigh curve may not apply

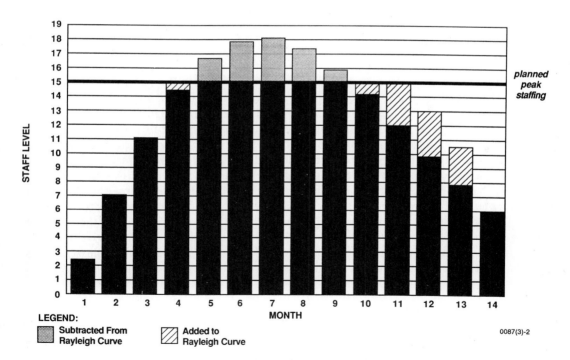

Figure 6–3.   Rayleigh curve–based staffing profile

universally, every organization has some limit on how fast it can accomplish a software job and needs to capture that information.

The optimum time to complete the project is a useful overview piece of knowledge, but it often must be supplemented by a more detail-level schedule. The purposes of the detail-level schedule are to establish well-defined points at which progress toward the overall schedule may be monitored and also to make a credibility check on the overall schedule estimate. Often, this detail-level schedule is established by defining the set of tasks to be performed during the project, allocating specific dates to each task based on working backward from the overall completion date using task-specific estimates, and seeing if the actual start date is consistent with the resultant "need" start date. For this purpose, it will be necessary to collect historic data not just at the overall project level but also at the task level—for example, detail design of an X subsystem of a Y application tends to take Z person months. Once again, an organization *must* collect historic data in order to make informed software estimates.

6-4 MONITOR PERFORMANCE

Because initial cost estimates are made so early in the software life cycle, they must be updated periodically (usually at each major milestone). Based on the eight projects studied, good designs cost about the same as poor ones. However, after completion of system design, additional information becomes available for refining cost and size estimates. For example, the count of units from a structure chart provides a better indication of final system size than is available from requirements. In particular, measuring complexity helps predict the amount and type of testing required. More complex systems require more testing, other things being equal.

Figure 6–4 shows that each one-point increase in system complexity produces about a one-percentage-point increase in the amount of testing effort required. The correlation coefficient of 0.65 is not quite significant. However, both projects that deviated from the trend required substantially more testing effort than expected (based on complexity considerations alone). Many factors could explain that.

Although this topic requires further study, measuring complexity holds the potential for providing the information necessary to focus testing efforts. The relative magnitude of structural, data, and procedural complexity suggest the probable distribution of errors during testing. Structural complexity means interface errors; data complexity means data and logic errors; excess procedural complexity means more logic errors. Software testing can be structured accordingly.

6-5 SUMMARY

The keys to accurate cost estimation are understanding the magnitude of the job to be done (software size) and the performance of the developing organization (productivity). An effective measurement program—gathering, analyzing, and utilizing

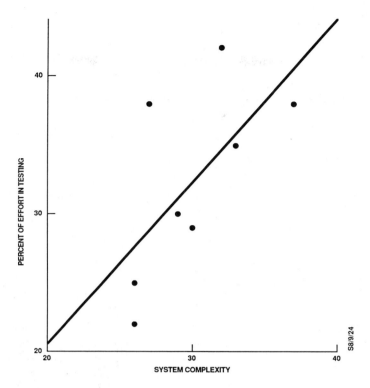

Figure 6-4. Complexity increases testing effort required

historic data—helps to achieve this understanding. Models are useful for comparison across organizations and when no data are available. However, no general model can substitute for the specific understanding of the job and its environment that measurement facilitates.

For project estimation purposes, a measurement program should focus on quantifying those factors that affect productivity in the local environment. For example, many of the 15 COCOMO factors will remain relatively constant for all projects within the same organization over a short (say, five years) period. It is not necessary to measure regularly those constant factors. To obtain the full benefit of a measurement program, the measures as well as the models in which they are applied must be kept and calibrated for each software enterprise.

Because there are a large number of estimation techniques, and because the choice among those techniques is application- and organization-dependent, it is not possible here to give specific advice on what data to collect and how to use the data once collected. But we have noted the types of data that might be collected and the uses those data can be put to. For further thoughts on specific data collection and use, see the references cited in this chapter.

7

Software Quality Control

Many software enterprises have quality assurance (or product assurance) organizations, but few practice quality control. Quality assurance consists of a set of techniques and procedures for identifying problems (instances of poor quality) in software *products* and ensuring that they are resolved. Most organizations try to make quality as high as possible, without ever measuring what level has been achieved, except perhaps to say that 100% conformance to standards was obtained.

On the other hand, product defects originate from people problems and methodology problems—in other words, *process* problems. Quality control consists of comparing observed quality with expected quality, then correcting the source of problems (the process) to bring quality back within an acceptable range. Quality control minimizes effort expended in rework by controlling the sources of defects. Measurement makes quality control possible.

Figure 7–1 illustrates the relationship between quality assurance and quality control. Typically, the product assurance organization performs a quality observation (inspection) and reporting function. Developers fix defects. Project management institutes corrective actions to the software development process necessary to prevent defects. Whereas quality control involves the entire software development

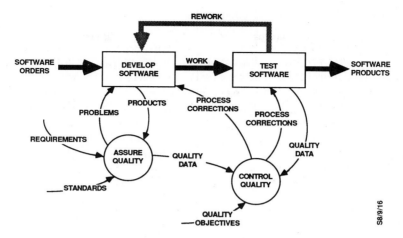

Figure 7-1. Software quality control model

organization, the quality assurance function belongs to the product assurance office.

Although this is a book on measurement, not quality assurance, some discussion of the software review process is necessary to explain the use of quality measures in this context (see [65] for an extensive guide for planning and performing software quality assurance). The following sections show how measurement supplements the quality assurance function to achieve control of the software design and implementation process. They describe the roles of measurement in design reviews, implementation quality control, and software acceptance.

7-1 SOFTWARE DESIGN ASSURANCE

Although software engineers are expected to produce a good design, the project manager still has responsibility for assessing that work in terms of satisfaction of requirements (traceability), ease of production (produceability), and conformance to standards. In a large project, no single individual can evaluate all these design attributes effectively.

Design reviews bring together participants with the expertise necessary to deal with these issues. The product assurance organization verifies compliance with standards. Managers question budgets and schedules. Technical personnel explain their approach to requirements satisfaction and produceability. The client describes his or her view of software requirements.

7-1-1 Design Review Objectives

Figure 7–2 shows the context of a generic software review. The reviewers compare a software product against predetermined criteria, then develop actions to address identified problems. The specific criteria used, and the form of the results produced, depend on the type of product being reviewed. From a measurement point of view, the design review is a data collection and analysis process.

At each step of design (and development), management needs to know not just how much work has been completed but also the quality of the work relative to the objectives of satisfaction of requirements, ease of production, and conformance to standards. Only "satisfactory" work should be reported as complete. Corrective actions must be developed to rectify process and product deficiencies.

Satisfaction of requirements.   During design, satisfaction of requirements can only be demonstrated by showing the traceability of requirements to design components, using techniques like those described by Mathur [50]. Generally, this attribute is measured in binary terms: Yes, it satisfies a particular requirement; or no, it does not. Requirements satisfaction may be measured as the percentage of requirements traceable to design. Software developers aim for complete satisfaction of functional and performance requirements, unless otherwise directed by the client. Usually, each departure from the requirements must be approved separately.

Evaluation of traceability and requirements satisfaction is often called verification and validation (V&V). Although the V&V role of software product assurance is essential to project success, it is not the focus of this book (see [65] for further discussion of this topic).

Conformance to standards.   Most organizations rely on standards to help ensure satisfaction of requirements and ease of production in the completed design. Although a standard notation by itself improves understandability and communication among software developers, concern for standards compliance can eclipse the

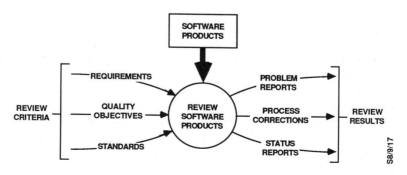

Figure 7–2.   Context of software product review

technical quality the standards were intended to promote. Glass [7] recommends relying on a small core of key standards rather than volumes of detail, with supplemental guidelines as helping hints but not as hard requirements.

Standards are a crude mechanism that can never substitute for technical understanding of the design process and application area. Their popularity derives from their easy implementation as checklists and forms. Some software enterprises view product assurance exclusively as a mechanism for verifying conformance to standards. (See [65] for more insight into the role of standards in software development.)

Achievement of produceability objectives.   Organizations develop quantitative objectives for produceability based on previous experience with other projects or earlier experience with the same project. Developing quantitative quality objectives requires systematic measurement. Failure to achieve (or even formulate) produceability objectives may result in a failure to satisfy budget and schedule constraints.

Produceability objectives relate to complexity, error rates, and rework effort. During a design review or inspection, participants should determine whether or not quality goals are being met. Use the figures of merit defined in this book. The guidelines and standards described above also provide reference points for comparison.

Reporting review results.   Unless review results are captured, the review effort has been wasted. Potential outputs of a design review include problem reports, corrective actions, and budget/schedule status information. Properly captured (recorded), these are measurements that can be used to evaluate the design process and product relative to expectations and past performance. Properly archived, they can later be used for new project planning and analysis.

Problem reports identify defects that must be corrected by the developers. These may be poorly conceived design, requirements discrepancies, or standards nonconformances. All problem reports must be recorded and tracked to completion. However, the results of a review should include more than just a list of problems. Corrective actions must both solve problems and attempt to eliminate the sources of problems (or counter their effects downstream). Corrective actions take the form of problem repair, insertion of new technology, changes in procedures, redefinitions of responsibilities, and resource reallocations. Only the project manager can impose a process-oriented corrective action.

Ultimately, the project manager needs to know whether or not the project is on the track to successful completion. This means comparing actual project status with budgets and schedules. Most approaches to performance measurement track work performed and resources expended but fail to capture any measure of the quality of the product. The software review process helps to make this assessment.

7-1-2 Design Review Schedule

Reviews and inspections should occur throughout the software life cycle. Table 7–1 shows the reviews, inspections, and audits prescribed by Computer Sciences Corporation's Digital System Development Methodology (DSDM)* [66]. However, the scope of this discussion will be confined to the role of measurement in the preliminary design review, critical design review, and unit design inspections.

Preliminary design review.   The preliminary design review (PDR) usually occurs after the functional allocation has been completed. The primary design concerns are the correct allocation of requirements to functions and definitions of external interfaces. Few standards exist for design products at this early stage. The most useful quantitative comparisons that can be made are with other similar systems. For example, are the numbers and types of functions proposed consistent with past experience in this application?

TABLE 7–1.   SOFTWARE PRODUCT ASSURANCE ACTIVITIES

SOFTWARE DEVELOPMENT PRODUCTS	LIFE-CYCLE PROCESS	RELEVANT BASELINE	CLIENT REVIEWS	INTERNAL INSPECTIONS	AUDITS
SOFTWARE REQUIREMENTS SPECIFICATION	Requirements Definition	Allocated	SSR or PDR	—	
Requirements Diagrams				Informal & PAO	Build and Acceptance
Function Specifications				Informal & PAO	
Data Dictionary				Informal & PAO	
ACCEPTANCE TEST PLAN	Design	N/A	PDR or CDR	—	Acceptance
PRELIMINARY SOFTWARE DESIGN SPECIFICATION		N/A	PDR	—	
Architecture Diagrams				Informal & PAO	N/A
Data Dictionary				Informal & PAO	
PRELIMINARY BUILD PLAN		N/A	PDR	—	
FINAL SOFTWARE DESIGN SPECIFICATION		Development and Product	CDR and BDR	—	
Architecture Diagrams				Walkthroughs	Build and Acceptance
Data Dictionary				Walkthroughs	
Users Manual				Walkthroughs	
FINAL BUILD PLAN		N/A	CDR and BDR	—	
BUILD TEST PLAN		N/A	CDR and BDR	—	Build
SOFTWARE UNITS	Implementation	N/A		—	
Designs		Product		Formal	
Test Plans		N/A		Formal	By PAO upon release for build testing
Code		Product		Informal	
Test Reports		N/A		Informal	
INTEGRATION TEST PLANS AND RESULTS		N/A	N/A	Informal	
SOFTWARE ENGINEERING NOTEBOOKS		N/A	N/A	—	
BUILD TEST PROCEDURES	Testing	N/A	N/A	Informal	
BUILD TEST REPORTS		N/A	N/A	Informal & PAO	Build
ACCEPTANCE TEST PROCEDURES		N/A	As produced	Informal	
ACCEPTANCE TEST REPORTS		N/A	As produced	Informal & PAO	Acceptance

DIRECTLY FROM S. STEPPEL, T. L. CLARK, et al., DIGITAL SYSTEM DEVELOPMENT METHODOLOGY, © 1984, P. 5-21. REPRINTED BY PERMISSION OF COMPUTER SCIENCES CORPORATION, SILVER SPRING, MD.

*DSDM is a registered trademark of Computer Sciences Corporation.

The initial cost and schedule estimates should be reviewed at this time too. If the PDR includes a high-level structure chart (or similar design representation), then the complexity issues (discussed below under the critical design review) can be addressed also.

Critical design review.   The critical design review (CDR) occurs after the system design has been completed. Again, the technical issues are traceability, produceability, and conformance to standards. Additionally, the manager should obtain the information necessary to determine budget/schedule status and update cost estimates.

For those adopting a structured design method, the system design should be represented as a fully developed structure chart and data dictionary. Many software enterprises prescribe standards for system design products. Traceability of requirements to design can be documented in a matrix. By following the main processing path through the system, the reviewers should encounter most of the requirements.

The results described in Chaps. 4 and 5 suggest that gradual modularization, where there are many levels in the calling structure, is best for produceability. Except in a few cases (like processing a set of alternative transactions), no unit should call more than three other application units. Whereas larger modules may facilitate development productivity, smaller modules promote maintainability. On the other hand, fault rate does not depend on module size but rather on relative complexity. During the critical design review, look for especially complex units, levels, or subsystems, as discussed earlier.

Examination of design profiles like those discussed in Sec. 5-3-3 helps to identify hierarchical levels where design decomposition has proceeded too rapidly. Similarly, unit complexity scores help to pinpoint problem areas. Overall, a good design aims to satisfy all requirements while minimizing complexity.

Many software development approaches require pseudocode for all units to be presented at CDR. This helps acquisition managers to be sure that "substantive" work has been done during the design phase. However, measurement makes it possible to evaluate a system design in terms of probable cost, maintainability, and error rate without accumulating reams of pseudocode at this stage. Use the functional, structural, and data complexity equations explained in Chap. 5 (calibrated for your organization) to assess the produceability of the design under review. Leave the development of pseudocode for implementation and subsequent review after CDR.

Unit design inspections.   The prolog and pseudocode of each unit developed should undergo a separate unit design inspection (UDI). This enables developers to adopt a true top-down incremental approach to implementation. The system design provides an overall structure within which programmers can design, code, and test individual units. Most organizations have standards prescribing structured programming methods for unit design and coding. The UDI should consider conformance to these standards, correctness of logic/data usage, and the adequacy of the unit test plan. Figure 7-3 illustrates this process. Fagan [67, 68] provides

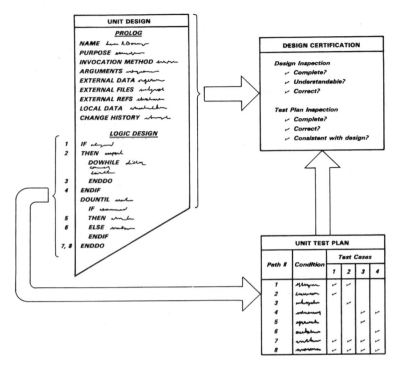

Figure 7-3. Typical unit design inspection procedure

extensive guidance for conducting UDIs. Note that the UDI is primarily a peer review process; in fact, as we move from CDR through PDR to UDI, we are also evolving from a management-focus review to a peer focus.

The data complexity equation from Chap. 5 (calibrated to your environment) can be used to estimate the number of decisions for each unit. Any unit whose pseudocode deviates very far from this target should be examined very carefully. If insufficient resources exist to inspect all units, then concentrate on inspecting the most complex units. Module size, in terms of lines of pseudocode, provides a crude indicator of complexity, but it should not be used to impose absolute limits on developers.

7-2 IMPLEMENTATION QUALITY CONTROL

As discussed earlier, achieving quality control requires measuring quality and comparing those measures with some expectation of the quality that should be achieved. In this section, we discuss *implementation* quality control—those quality control activities performed after CDR but before delivery of the software product for acceptance testing. Usually, a large project is implemented as a series of increasingly complete builds or releases.*

More than quality assurance, quality control requires up-front planning to define objectives and establish procedures, if it is to succeed. Complexity graphs and control charts (described below) are two basic techniques for defining expectations and comparing them with actual results during the software development process. Overall, the amount of rework effort experienced on a project indicates the effectiveness of an organization's product assurance/quality control mechanism.

Complexity graphs. Most design methods recommend trying several alternative designs before settling on one. Not only do designers not have the time to do this but such a procedure does not produce the most effective product. Good designs evolve, they don't appear by spontaneous generation in their final form. Unfortunately, designs often remain incomplete until late in the project. Design must be an iterative process. Measures provide a mechanism for guiding those iterations to a successful conclusion.

Figure 7–4 shows how the structural complexity of a stable design converges over time. The complexity added at each iteration (or milestone) is less than that added at the preceding iteration. After CDR, system complexity increases slowly. From PDR to CDR, system complexity increases by 83 percent, but from CDR to Release 2, it increases by only 31 percent. This indicates that the initial design is being ''filled in'' rather than added onto or dramatically restructured.

Whereas the design of Fig. 7–4 required more than 500 KSLOC to implement, only 30 system design changes were proposed. (This project comes from outside the SEL application area.) Note from the figure that other measures of design, like the number of units defined (to date), do not behave as smoothly as structural complexity. Figure 7–4 also provides an expected range of complexity for the next release of the project; each complexity increment should be less than the last. Sudden increases in complexity signal an unstable or seriously incomplete design.

The general availability and increasing use of design tools like Design Generator®, Excelerator®, and DesignAid® mean that designs are now often stored in a machine-readable format like source code. This makes design more amenable to analysis. However, the need for design analysis tools as add-ons or integrated into design packages has thus far gone largely unrecognized. In time, design analysis will become as much a part of software engineering as it is of civil engineering (for example).

Control charts. Measuring error rates during testing helps to determine whether or not the software development process is in control (stable). Many of the

---

*CSC's methodology [66] prescribes an incremental approach to developing large systems. A build is a partial but executable subset of the designed system. Build development (called ''implementation'') includes unit design/code/test and integration/system testing activities. A build that undergoes acceptance testing for delivery to the customer is termed a release.

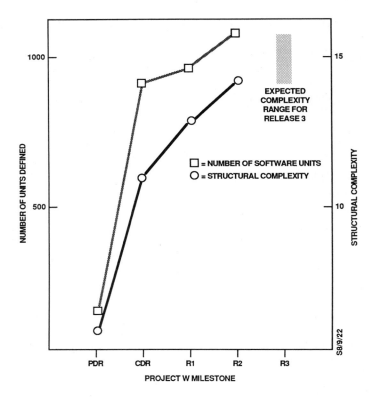

Figure 7-4. Example of complexity convergence

errors detected during system testing originate in system design. Unit design and coding errors should be screened out during unit design inspections, code reading, and unit testing. If they are not, then a corrective action is needed.

Dobbins [69] describes some "natural numbers of programming." One of these numbers is error rate (errors per 1,000 lines of code). Within a large project, the error rate tends to stabilize over time. Departures from this steady state of the development process should be scrutinized carefully. The control chart (a statistical process control technique [70]) provides one mechanism for monitoring process performance.

Figure 7-5 shows examples of control charts for the error rate. Error rates are plotted for each of seven releases of two projects. (These are FORTRAN projects from outside the SEL domain.) Note that the cumulative error rate for each project remains relatively stable, verifying the notion of "natural numbers." The figures also show upper and lower "control limits" based on local historical data for each release of each project. Crossing a control limit indicates that the project's software process has changed significantly.

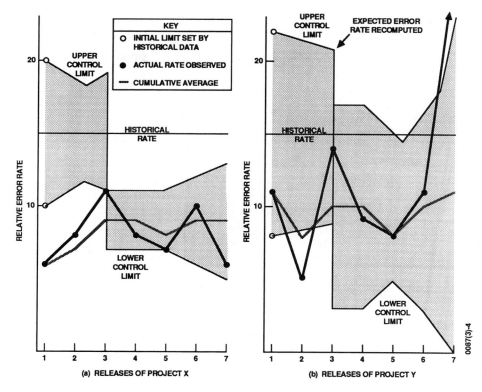

Figure 7–5. Sample control charts

Initially, both projects outperform the historical error rate. However, project Y (Figure 7–5b) goes off the chart (relative error rate of 42) on the seventh release. The cause of the problem must be found and corrected to bring performance back to an acceptable level. The control chart only indicates the presence of a process problem; it does not identify its nature. However, studying more detailed effectiveness measures (see below) may provide an answer.

Many different methods can be used to compute control limits for control charts [70]. In this example, control limits for the first releases are set three standard deviations from the historical error rate. After three releases, control limits are reset three standard deviations from the cumulative error rate from the initial releases. In general, control limits for error rates are defined as follows:

$$\text{Upper limit} = \tilde{u} + 3 \sqrt{\frac{\tilde{u}}{n}} \qquad (7\text{--}1)$$

$$\text{Lower limit} = \tilde{u} - 3 \sqrt{\frac{\tilde{u}}{n}} \qquad (7\text{--}2)$$

where

$\tilde{u}$ = cumulative or historical error rate
$\overline{n}$ = source lines of code tested (this release)

Thus, the control limits for project Y are wider because its releases are smaller (average release = 23 KSLOC) than those of project X (average release = 138 KSLOC). Note that project X begins production with performance significantly better than the historical rate. Its first three releases fall below the lower control limit. Subsequently, the control chart limits were adjusted to monitor the new level of performance.

Manufacturing organizations that have been using statistical process control techniques for a while have a good historical basis for setting the expected error rate ($\tilde{u}$). With software's short history and rapid rate of technology change, quality control techniques for software development must be applied carefully. However, measuring a project against itself circumvents the project manager's standard argument that the project is unique and shouldn't be measured. In addition to control limits, the analyst should watch for trends within the control limits as indicators of change [70].

Effectiveness measures.   Measuring the effectiveness of individual quality assurance procedures and of the entire program is an important component of quality control. Dunn [71] describes a simple effectiveness measure for individual activities:

$$E = \frac{N}{N + S} \qquad (7-3)$$

where

E = effectiveness of activity
N = number of faults (defects) found by activity
S = number of faults (defects) found by subsequent activities

This measure can be tuned by selecting only those faults (defects) present at the time of the activity and susceptible to detection by the activity [71]. Testing effectiveness (the percentage of all errors found in testing that were found in system testing) is one important such measure. The development manager needs to know how the testers are doing as well as how the programmers are doing. Like error rate, testing effectiveness can be analyzed with a control chart. Establishing a chain of effectiveness measures spanning the life cycle also supports process improvement goals (see also Chap. 8).

The percentage of effort spent in rework provides the best measure of the overall effectiveness of a quality assurance program. Estimates of rework in software development range from 30 to 50 percent (i.e., 30 to 50 percent of the total effort is spent on correcting problems). More errors means more rework. More rework means lower productivity. An effective quality assurance program will decrease rework effort over time. Unfortunately, most software enterprises are very sensitive about measuring rework effort because it tends to be a measure of "failure" rather than of "success."

Implementation quality control techniques (like complexity graphs and control charts), used in conjunction with design reviews and inspections, help the development manager to achieve the level of confidence and control necessary to ensure successful completion of a software project.

7-3 SOFTWARE ACCEPTANCE CRITERIA

An engineering approach to design based on figures of merit should lead to a better product. However, software acquisition managers still need objective criteria for determining whether or not the quality of the delivered software is acceptable, regardless of how it was developed. The first criterion must be: Does it satisfy functional and performance requirements? Product standards may also be imposed. Maintainability and confidence (reliability) must be taken into account too.

The acceptance decision must also consider the cost of rework that may be required to make the software acceptable (if rejected). The best way for an acquisition manager to promote acceptability of the final software product (and minimize the potential for rework) is to participate in the early stages of the project through reviews (as shown in Table 7–1).

This section explains some objective quality measures to consider when making an acceptance decision. In addition to complexity measures, the software acquisition manager should examine three other measures: test coverage, error rate, and unreferenced variables. These measures indicate the level of confidence and ease of maintenance that can be expected from the software.

Test coverage.   Calculations of confidence in software quality (error rate) assume that the software has been fully tested. Fully tested generally means that *all* requirements have been tested and that some fairly high percentage (60 to 90 percent) of structure has been tested. The amount of structure tested can be measured. In fact, without this measurement it is nearly impossible to know how effective the testing process has been. The notion of test coverage is related to cyclomatic complexity (see Sec. 3-2). The most popular criterion for test coverage is to ensure that all outcomes of all decisions (and thus all reachable statements) have been tested [72]. This requires a dynamic analyzer (a commercially available tool) to track test execution.

Test coverage may be measured both at the unit test level and on the fully integrated system. Unit test measurement determines intramodule test coverage; integration test measurement can then focus on intermodule coverage. Because interactions of units cannot be observed during unit testing alone, test coverage measured during unit testing does not provide evidence of "complete" testing.

Even if test cases are only functionally (not structurally) based, the level of test coverage achieved during testing should be measured and reported because test coverage is an excellent measure of test thoroughness.

Error rate.   The software acquisition manager usually wants an estimate of the number of errors remaining in the system (or the error rate). That depends on the number of errors originally in the system and the effectiveness of the system testing process. Much research in using mean time between failures and error correction rates to predict software reliability has been done, but there is still a lot of theoretical and practical uncertainty about these statistical models.

Figure 7–6 shows a simple model of the error discovery process. During system testing, 100 percent coverage of the software should be attained. As test coverage increases, more errors emerge. The number of errors found during system testing establishes a lower bound for the total number of errors in the system. Experience shows that conscientious system testing (for noncritical software) uncovers about 80 percent of the total errors eventually found. Typically, 20 percent remain to be found during acceptance testing and operation (the "d" in Fig. 7–6).

A quick test for software quality can be made by computing the portion of the 20 percent of errors (expected during acceptance testing and operations) that

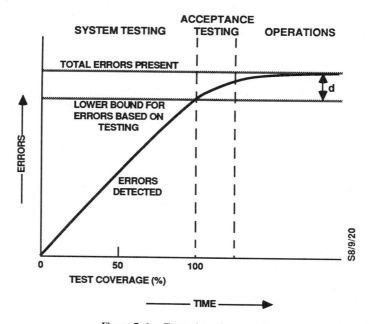

Figure 7–6.   Error detection model

are found during acceptance testing alone. If the system exceeds this quota during acceptance testing, it's in trouble. This test works better when based on appropriate historical data.

Usually, acceptance testing does not achieve 100 percent coverage of the software. In that case the formulas for control limits—Eqs. (7–1) and (7–2)—can be used to compute confidence limits for the error rate observed during testing. Note that confidence improves as more software is tested (n) but declines as the error rate ($\bar{u}$) increases (standard deviation (σ) = $\sqrt{\bar{u}/n}$). The equivalent lines of code tested (n) can be approximated by multiplying total lines of code delivered by the test coverage achieved.

The probability that the true error rate differs from the error rate observed during testing depends on the standard deviation. For example, a 95 percent confidence interval extends for two standard deviations (2σ) on both sides of the observed error rate. Assuming that all discovered problems will be fixed without introducing new errors, the standard deviation measures the risk (due to undiscovered problems) involved in accepting the software "as is."

Thus, the software acquisition manager should formulate error rate acceptance criteria in terms of both a maximum acceptable error rate and the probability that the true error rate exceeds that value. That is, acceptance criteria for error rate should take the form: the probability that the true error rate exceeds one error per 1,000 source lines must be less than 1 percent, for example. Appropriate error rate limits and confidence levels must be set by the acquisition manager.

Recent advances in statistical testing techniques based on random testing [73] make possible more accurate estimation of the true error rate and reliability. However, these techniques require changes in requirements and design methods to define the sample space for test case selection. If the operational scenario is well understood, and testing is structured to reflect operations, then statistical testing and reliability models can provide an indication of software reliability in operation.

Unreferenced variables. Figure 7–7 presents some results of a study of the relationship of the presence of unreferenced variables in a module to its fault rate [45]. Keeping logically related variables together in COMMON, even when all modules do not use them all, appeared to be beneficial. However, unreferenced variables from other sources indicated problems. Figure 7–7 shows that those modules with a high percentage of unreferenced locally defined and calling sequence variables are fault-prone (consistent with the complexity model of Chap. 5). The values in the figure exclude unreferenced COMMON variables.

These unreferenced variables arise because of poor design, programmer error, or as a correction to an error (an erroneous/unnecessary reference is removed). In any event, Fig. 7–7 shows that the presence of unreferenced variables indicates sloppy design and/or coding. The software acquisition manager should require evidence of additional testing or other verification of modules with many unreferenced variables.

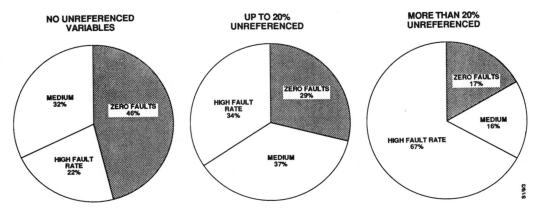

Figure 7–7.   Fault rate by unreferenced variables

Software complexity.   Ease of maintenance is the other major issue concerning software acquisition managers. Chapter 5 demonstrated the relationship of procedural complexity to maintainability. Because simpler (smaller) modules promote maintainability, the software acquisition manager may want to limit the acceptable level of procedural complexity in some way. However, that must be done carefully to avoid unintended side effects like increasing the error rate.

Small modules are a consequence of good design rather than a primary criterion for achieving good design. A software design composed of small modules achieved by rapid decomposition (producing high structural complexity) without regard to functionality is a bad design. Thus, an effective limit on procedural complexity requires a corresponding limit on structural complexity.

Figure 7–8 shows how the contributions of structural and data complexity to error rate combine to define an optimum size for modules in terms of procedural (cyclomatic) complexity. Remember that procedural complexity is a (nondeterministic) function of data complexity. Unless restrained, the software developer can easily lower procedural complexity by driving up structural complexity. Note the general similarity of the hypothetical distribution of error rate in Fig. 7–8 to the empirical distribution of Fig. 4–1.

Optimum complexity depends on factors like programming language and application type. Setting a complexity maximum far below this optimum may adversely affect the software development activity, resulting in error-prone software. Moreover, some modules cannot be efficiently implemented without exceeding the maximum complexity unless it is set very high.

Thus, acceptance criteria for procedural complexity should be set in statistical rather than absolute terms (i.e., specify that no more than 5 percent of delivered modules can exceed the acceptance limit). Moreover, a structural complexity limit should accompany the procedural complexity criteria. Establishing appropriate acceptance criteria for an application and environment requires experience and sys-

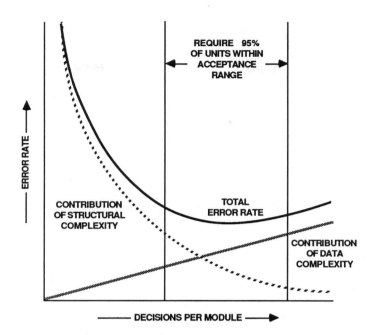

Figure 7-8. Acceptance criteria for procedural complexity

tematic measurement. Stating the acceptance criteria in statistical terms allows developers to use their best engineering judgment while still constraining their overall performance.

7-4 SUMMARY

This chapter explained some measurement techniques that assist the manager in controlling software projects. To apply these techniques, the development manager needs to track the complexity measures described in Chap. 5 as well as error rate, testing efficiency, and test coverage. The acquisition manager needs to determine structural complexity, procedural complexity, test coverage, error rate, and unreferenced variables.

This chapter introduced the important concept of quality control. Controlling quality means setting quantitative quality objectives, measuring project performance against the objectives, and then taking corrective action as needed to bring performance back into line with the objectives. Measurement makes quality control possible.

Specifically, this chapter suggested that the manager responsible for a quality product do the following:

1. Use design reviews (preliminary, critical, unit) to demonstrate
   a. Satisfaction of requirements (via traceability of all or some percentage of requirements to design components)
   b. Ease of production (via the figures of merit discussed in Chap. 5)
   c. Conformance to standards (via a minimal but enforceable set of standards)
2. Use implementation quality control in the form of
   a. Complexity graphs (to ensure that complexity grows gradually and that growth diminishes with time)
   b. Control charts (to ensure that various key factors, such as error rate, evolve within historic and predicted limits)
   c. Effectiveness measures (to ensure that an activity achieves its expected performance—e.g., fault detection during code review as a percentage of total faults, or rework activity versus historic rework activity)
3. Use software acceptance criteria such as
   a. Test coverage measures
   b. Counting errors found during the acceptance process and unreferenced variables in the source code to determine if the counts are within historic bounds
   c. Statistical testing and reliability models if the operational scenario is well understood
   d. The complexity measures discussed in Chap. 5.

These quantitative techniques supplement the manager's expert judgment to help him or her do a better job.

8

Software Process Analysis

Doing a better job each time is part of doing a good job. Measuring the course of software development and consequences of design provides the information necessary to improve progressively the software process within an organization. Tools, methods, measures, and standards all must be customized to achieve optimum performance within any software enterprise. Practitioners cannot be sure that a new technology works in their environment, or that they are using it correctly, until they themselves have measured its effects. The general steps to process improvement [16] are

- Measure and analyze current performance to establish a process baseline and identify leverage points.
- Innovate and evaluate benefits of new technology in the production setting.
- Transfer proven technology to practitioners throughout the software enterprise.

Whereas the last step lies beyond the scope of this book, the first two rely extensively on software measurement, as discussed below.

8-1 PROCESS LEVERAGE POINTS

The software enterprise's methodology, together with its tool support, defines its process. The analyst must repeatedly pose five basic questions about the set of activities that comprise this process [81, pp. 117–118]:

1. Is this activity necessary, or can it be eliminated?
2. Can this activity be combined with another?
3. Is this the proper sequence of activities?
4. Can this activity be improved?
5. Is the proper person doing this activity?

For most software processes, these questions suggest many opportunities for improvement. Measurement provides the tools to identify critical problem areas in current performance. The Pareto principle predicts that, in general, 20 percent of causes generate 80 percent of problems. Finding and eliminating that 20 percent can deliver significant productivity and quality benefits. Although major process problems may not always be that obvious, problems usually are concentrated in a few areas. These areas are the leverage points for process improvement.

Figure 8–1 illustrates the use of histograms to identify major sources of errors. The chart classifies 590 errors from one medium-scale project. Interface errors account for one-third of all errors. Only 17 percent of errors relate to initialization and computation, the classes of errors most likely to originate during coding. In this example, an appropriate process improvement would be to institute unit design inspections (which were not performed for this project).

After a problem area has been identified, strategies to improve that process element can be implemented. Some basic strategies for software process improvement include automating manual activities, increasing software reuse, and reducing rework (through improved verification). Potential process improvements must also be evaluated in cost-benefit terms. Items that offer only marginal improvement at high cost may be deferred.

Almost all the measures listed in Fig. 2–3 are useful for capturing and evaluating the software process performance baseline. They provide visibility into the process that is not provided by gross measures of productivity and error rate. As an example, an increase in the error rate on one project may be related to an unusual volume of design changes. In another case, high productivity may be achieved by extensively reusing existing units. The process engineer needs this information to understand and improve the software process.

8-2 SOFTWARE TECHNOLOGY EVALUATION

The actual productivity and quality effect of process changes (usually new technology) cannot be taken for granted. Each technology innovation must be evaluated.

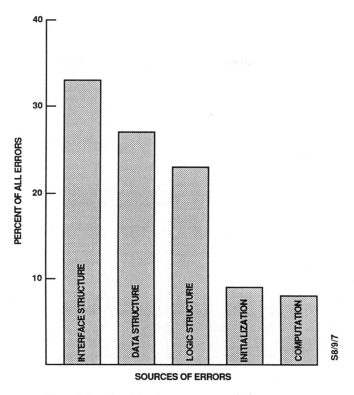

Figure 8-1. Example of error source analysis

Software researchers commonly apply three approaches to experimentation and evaluation [82]:

- *Case study*—an in-depth comparison of two projects (one with new technology), without making statistical inferences.
- *Multiproject variation*—general measurement and analysis of varying levels of technology across a large number of projects.
- *Controlled experiment*—selection and control of subjects, tasks, methods, and environments according to a formal statistical design. Because of its prohibitive cost in a production environment, the controlled experiment usually, and unfortunately, is conducted in a classroom setting with student subjects.

However, a fourth type of analysis, the process experiment, can also be applied in production environments. When the process is in statistical control, improvements can be readily detected by comparison with the performance baseline. Figure 8-2

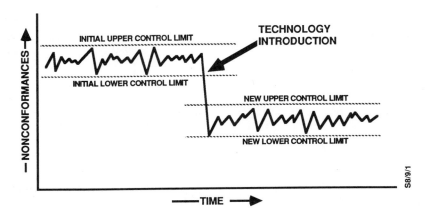

Figure 8-2. Technology innovation example

illustrates the effect of an innovation on quality as tracked by a control chart. Although effects may not always be this dramatic, real improvements are measurable.

Sayward [74] recommends at least two trials of a new technology in a pattern of introduction/withdrawal/introduction to ensure that any observed effect is not the result of other factors such as learning or the Hawthorne effect. Actually, it's easier to do this in a project-oriented environment like software development than in a continuous assembly line.

Clearly, using the process experiment as a tool for process improvement requires, first, achieving quality control. Although this may seem like an unnecessary delay to those wishing to be on the road to immediate order-of-magnitude increases in productivity, a little reflection suggests that inserting new technology into an unstable and uncontrolled process is more likely to lead to further instability than sustained improvement.

Once a new technology has proven itself, transfer to practitioners at large can be made by providing appropriate methods, tools, and training. Over time, a software enterprise with a successful process improvement program will be able to document trends toward lower error rate, reduced rework, and increased productivity. As an example, Card et al. [75] provide a general discussion of the measurement-oriented productivity and quality improvement program at Computer Sciences Corporation.

8-3 SUMMARY

Improving the design and implementation *process* leads to improvement in software and design *product* quality. Taking a systematic approach to software process improvement means first defining the process and establishing quality control, then continually modifying the process to improve its performance over time. Modifying the process involves analyzing the baseline, evaluating new technology, and transitioning changes (including new technology) to practitioners throughout the organization. Measurement plays a key role in software process improvement.

9
Concluding Remarks

The past eight chapters covered quite a lot of material in a short space. They outlined general principles, made recommendations, described examples, and explained numerical techniques. Their purpose has been to establish a conceptual framework for collecting and applying software measures. Many details remain to be filled in. This last chapter reviews some commonly encountered obstacles to software measurement practice and then offers a perspective on the present and future role of measurement in software engineering.

9-1 OBSTACLES TO MEASUREMENT

Effective measurement derives from theory and supports practice. The measurement practitioner must understand what he or she is trying to measure, and why, to have any hope of success. Collecting miscellaneous measures does not necessarily lead to this understanding. The successful measurement program incorporates carefully selected measures that respond to organizational needs.

Once an organization begins collecting measures, it often collects too many. It is better to use a few measures that are well understood rather than many measures that are not. A large volume of data does not substitute for understanding. Too much data often lead to casual analysis instead of serious study.

Another key to operating a successful measurement program is knowing what to expect from measures. Measurement identifies problems, it does not solve them. Measurement does not substitute for effective management, engineering methods, product assurance, or software testing. However, it can improve the effectiveness of all those activities.

Selecting from among the available measurement ideas poses another set of practical problems. Measures never die. For example, Halstead measures still appear in new software tools, in spite of the very convincing evidence against them (see Chap. 3). Rely on measures that clearly relate to organizational activities. Don't propose measures that initially require drastic changes in the organization or operation of the software enterprise; management will never approve that.

Software managers, tool vendors, methodologists, and the like do not really want objective measurement. Most of these people are comfortable with a system that puts a premium on presentation rather than performance. Software acquisition managers and software engineers are the ones calling for better measures. The greatest challenge in measurement practice is convincing management to want measurement in the first place.

9-2 MEASUREMENT AND THE PRESENT

Experience suggests that the success of a software enterprise depends on consistently satisfying four "technical" conditions. Other managerial considerations (like getting new business and keeping key employees) are also essential. The four technical conditions are

1. Understanding the customer's requirements
2. Getting a "good" design
3. Implementing that design in a controlled incremental fashion
4. Improving the software process over time

Measurement helps to achieve these conditions. The software cost estimation exercise tests the engineer's understanding of the requirements. Although many issues may remain unresolved at this stage, conscientious attention to the estimation process helps to identify areas of ambiguity. Complexity measures assist the designer in converging on a good solution. Quality control techniques help the manager to keep the implementation process tuned. Process analysis provides the information necessary to improve enterprise performance over time.

Most software enterprises now collect some minimal set of data to support their cost estimation efforts. Figure 2–3 identified a larger set of measures that support the wider range of measurement applications proposed here. The cost of collecting these data should not exceed 1 percent of software development cost. That can easily be recaptured through improved software development performance. The act of measurement, itself, improves performance consciousness.

Measurement for cost estimation has succeeded because both the theoretical concepts and practical objectives are clear. The methods have been refined through extensive practical experience. This book explains the results of adopting a similar approach to measuring software design quality. Quality models, like cost models, must be calibrated to fit each environment. And, as in cost estimation, there is room for more than one model.

9-3 MEASUREMENT AND THE FUTURE

Measurement will become more important in the future of software engineering. Chapter 1 pointed out the key role of measurement in moving the level of quality assurance technology from inspection to control to engineering. Current software research focuses on developing alternative life cycle paradigms (Agresti [76] provides a good summary) and on design automation through expert systems and artificial intelligence (as described by Balzer et al. [77]). However, the success of both endeavors depends to some extent on improved measures.

Software measurement is the key to freeing the software development process from lockstep with the waterfall life cycle model. Shaw [78] argues that the major recent advance in software engineering practice has been in the improvement of management based on this model. Alternatives to the lockstep waterfall model will not become widely accepted until managers can be sure of retaining control of the new process. Managers have to know how much of the job has been done and whether or not the work is any good. This requires objective measures of quality and production.

Reliable measures also are essential to design automation. Major software research centers are investing their long-term hopes for software process improvement in artificial intelligence and expert systems. However, no process can be automated before it is well understood, measurable, and controllable. We have to achieve "natural" intelligence before "artificial" intelligence becomes meaningful. Design automation cannot occur without effective design measurement techniques.

9-4 MEASUREMENT AND GOALS

In this book we have toured the world of software design from a measurement point of view. First we developed a set of principles (Part I) underlying and exhibiting the importance of measurement and data collection. Then we examined the application of those principles—the use of measurement results in both software design (Part II) and software management (Part III). As our understanding of this point of view increased, certain key design measurement goals and design measures emerged. In Fig. 2–3, we summarized those design measures. Here, in these final tables of the book (Tables 9–1 and 9–2), we focus on those goals and their achievement through the measures.

Table 9–1 lists the several goals we have discussed throughout the book—maximizing produceability, improving estimation, and strengthening management—and

TABLE 9–1. A GOAL-ORIENTED VIEW OF SOFTWARE DESIGN QUALITY MEASURES

TECHNIQUE	MEASURE	CHAPTER WHERE DISCUSSED	STRIVE FOR ...
GOAL: MAXIMIZE PRODUCEABILITY			
COMPLEXITY ANALYSIS	FANOUT	5	THREE OR FEWER MODULES; DEEP RATHER THAN BROAD CALL STRUCTURE
	NUMBER OF I/O VARIABLES PER MODULE	5	REDUCE TO ESSENTIAL MINIMUM
	FANOUT; NUMBER OF I/O VARIABLES; NUMBER OF MODULES	5	PLOT OF THESE SHOULD RESULT IN SIMILAR, S-SHAPED CURVES
MAXIMIZE STRENGTH	FUNCTIONS PER MODULE	4	FEW FUNCTIONS/MODULE; RELATED FUNCTIONS
GOAL: IMPROVE ESTIMATION			
HISTORIC DATA (BOTH ORIGINAL AND ACTUAL)	LINES OF CODE AND/OR FUNCTION POINTS VERSUS APPLICATION DOMAIN	6	DATA USEFUL FOR FUTURE ESTIMATES
	PRODUCTIVITY ADJUSTMENT VERSUS APPLICATION DOMAIN	6	MORE ACCURATE PRODUCTIVITY ADJUSTMENT FOR CALCULATING EFFORT (SECTION 6.2)
	ADJUSTMENT CONSTANTS A AND B	6	MORE ACCURATE WORK BREAKDOWN DEFINITION (SECTION 6.3)
	EFFORT BY LIFE-CYCLE TASK	6	MORE ACCURATE WORK BREAKDOWN STRUCTURE HISTORY (SECTION 6.3)
GOAL: STRENGTHEN MANAGEMENT			
COMPLEXITY GRAPHS	COMPLEXITY	3, 7	GRADUAL AND DIMINISHING GROWTH OF COMPLEXITY
CONTROL CHARTS	ERRORS PER 1000 LINES OF CODE*; HISTORIC AND CURRENT	7	CURRENT NUMBERS WITHIN ENVELOPE OF HISTORIC AND/OR PROJECTED CURRENT PROJECT DATA
EFFECTIVENESS MEASURES	DEFECTS PER ACTIVITY; REWORK TIME; HISTORY AND CURRENT	7	MINIMAL VALUES BUT ALSO VALUES WITHIN ENVELOPE OF HISTORIC DATA
	TEST COVERAGE	7	MAXIMIZE PERCENT OF STRUCTURE TESTED (WITHIN COST CONSTRAINTS)
	ACCEPTANCE TEST DETECTED ERRORS; HISTORIC AND CURRENT	7	MINIMAL VALUES, BUT ALSO VALUES WITHIN ENVELOPE OF HISTORIC DATA
	UNREFERENCED VARIABLES	7	MINIMAL VALUES, BUT ALSO VALUES WITHIN ENVELOPE OF HISTORIC DATA
PROCESS** ANALYSIS	BASELINE VERSUS CURRENT PERFORMANCE: DESIGN CHANGES, STANDARDS, NON-CONFORMANCES, MODIFIED UNITS, REUSED UNITS, PAGES OF DOCUMENTATION	8	PROCESS CHANGES THAT PRODUCE MEASUREABLE IMPROVEMENT

0168S(4)-13

* THIS SAME TECHNIQUE CAN BE USEFUL FOR OTHER MEASURES.

** USE PARETO ANALYSIS TO IDENTIFY MEASURES OF CONCERN IN A PARTICULAR LOCAL PROJECT OR ENTERPRISE.

TABLE 9–2. SURPRISE CONCLUSIONS ENCOUNTERED IN THIS BOOK

CONCLUSION	CHAPTER
SOFTWARE ENGINEERING WITHOUT MEASUREMENT IS NOT ENGINEERING	1
A SOFTWARE ENTERPRISE CAN COLLECT TOO MUCH DATA	2
SOFTWARE SCIENCE MEASURES DO NOT APPEAR TO HAVE PRACTICAL USEFULNESS	3
STANDARDS THAT ARBITRARILY LIMIT MODULE SIZE SEEM TO BE ILL-ADVISED	4
COMMON COUPLING IS NOT AS BAD AS WE THOUGHT	4, 5
FANOUT SHOULD BE SMALLER THAN WE THOUGHT	4,5
PRODUCTIVITY NUMBERS ARE OFTEN CRUDE AND MAY BE MISLEADING	5
DELIVERED SOURCE INSTRUCTIONS ARE NOT ALWAYS A GOOD MEASURE OF WORK	5, 6
STANDARDS ARE OFTEN TOO COMPREHENSIVE	7
UNIQUE PROJECTS CAN STILL BE MEASURED AGAINST THEMSELVES	7
TEST COVERAGE IS A VITAL BUT SELDOM-USED MEASURE	7
UNREFERENCED VARIABLES ARE A GOOD INDICATOR OF TROUBLE	7
MEASUREMENT MAKES PRODUCTIVITY AND QUALITY IMPROVEMENT MEANINGFUL	8

0168S(4)-16

makes some very specific suggestions about measures that will help us achieve those goals. The table also shows where more information can be obtained about measures in this book, and what we should strive for when we work with them. This table thus becomes a kind of action reference summary for the ideas developed more fully earlier in the book.

Table 9–2 is a different kind of summary. As we explored SEL and other project data for measures to help us achieve our goals, we encountered some surprises along the way. It has become apparent that there are some old wives' tales in the software engineering profession and that not all of them are supportable when confronted with real project data. In this table, those surprises are summarized for future reference.

Software engineering is not engineering unless there is measurement. That was our position as we began the discussions in this book. We hope, now that the presentation is concluded, that you will agree. And we also hope that that agreement will result in a commitment to explore the world of software design measurement on your own, perhaps using these ideas as an effective starting point.

Appendix A
Recommended Reading

This appendix points to a few key sources that the software measurement practitioner will want to keep at hand. Many good books on software engineering and statistics are available; understanding these concepts and techniques is essential to developing an effective software measurement program. In addition, some specialized knowledge will help.

Boehm, B. W., *Software Engineering Economics.* Englewood Cliffs, N.J.: Prentice-Hall, 1981. No more comprehensive treatment of software cost estimation exists than this. Boehm quantifies the effects of many different productivity and quality factors and explains his own and other cost models. Every technical library should have a copy of this book. Every software measurement practitioner will need access to this material. Cost estimators will want to have their own copy. However, its great length means that few will manage to read it in its entirety.

DeMarco, T., *Controlling Software Projects.* Englewood Cliffs, N.J.: Prentice-Hall, 1982. DeMarco describes a much more detailed technical and management approach to software measurement than is presented in this book, and he covers a wider range of topics than Boehm. Those measurement practitioners planning to expand beyond the foundations established here should acquire and study DeMarco's book. It discusses many important issues and provides many stimulating ideas. DeMarco also includes a brief appendix on statistical concepts.

Grady, R. B., and **D. L. Caswell,** *Software Metrics: Establishing a Company-wide Program.* Englewood Cliffs, N.J.: Prentice-Hall, 1988. The authors describe the introduction and evolution of a software measurement program at Hewlett-Packard. The book deals effectively with people issues like getting managers and engineers to accept measurement, how to prepare reports, what training is needed, and so on. The book is rather sketchy, however, about how to use measurement to make engineering and management decisions. It is a good complement to the present text. Whereas the overall philosophy of measurement is similar, the topics discussed are mostly different (but also essential to measurement success).

Pyzdek, T., *An SPC (Statistical Process Control) Primer.* Tuscon, AZ: Quality America, 1978. Pyzdek defines elementary statistical concepts and explains some simple techniques for evaluating and controlling process performance. Developed originally for manufacturing and customer service processes, the concepts are readily applicable to software development. Every software measurement practitioner (in particular those involved in quality assurance) should have a copy of this inexpensive book or its equivalent. Recently, general statistics texts have begun to include some coverage of statistical process control.

Schulmeyer, G.G., and **J. I. McManus,** eds., *Handbook of Software Quality Assurance.* New York: Van Nostrand Reinhold, 1987. The editors have collected 17 articles by software quality assurance (SQA) experts who describe a practical approach to SQA based on their own extensive experience. The specific topics discussed include design reviews, inspections, configuration management, data analysis, statistical testing, program organization, and personnel requirements. Every product assurance practitioner should have a copy of this or a similar reference.

Appendix B

Design Complexity Profiles

This appendix presents system design profiles (as explained in Sec. 5-3-3) for each of the eight SEL projects analyzed. Each figure (B–1 through B–8) plots the cumulative percentage of modules, fanout (control), and I/O variables (data) by hierarchical level for one project. A standard user interface occupies level 1 of all systems.

These figures simplify the design structure by combining all utility modules, regardless of where invoked, into a single deepest level of the design. ("Utility" refers to new or reused modules that are invoked from more than one other module but are not standard or system utilities.) Levels greater than or equal to 10 are also combined into a single level to facilitate plotting.

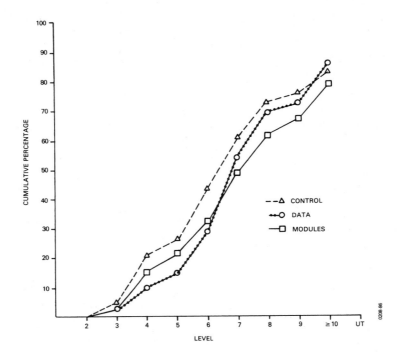

Figure B-1. Project A profile

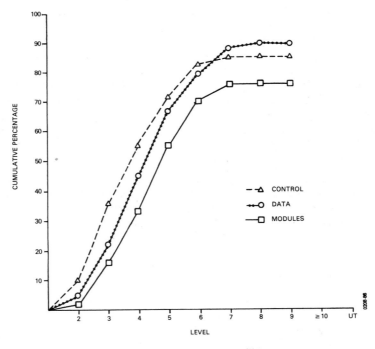

Figure B-2. Project B profile

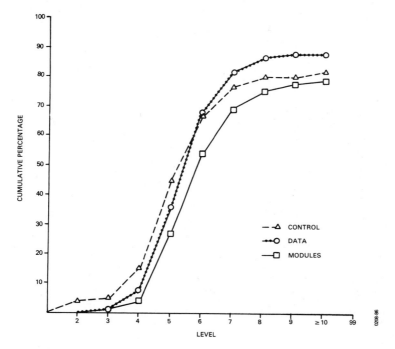

Figure B-3. Project C profile

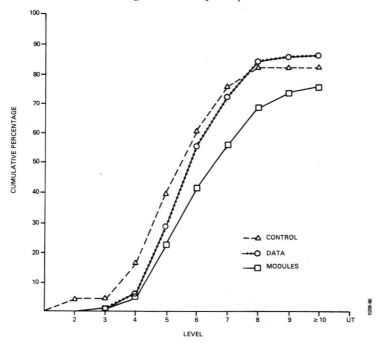

Figure B-4. Project D profile

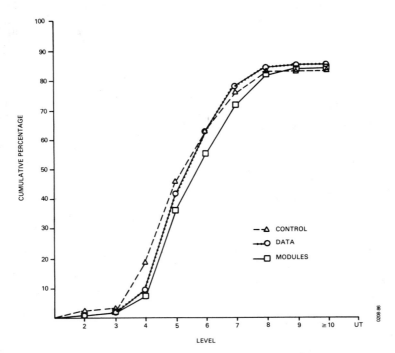

Figure B-5. Project E profile

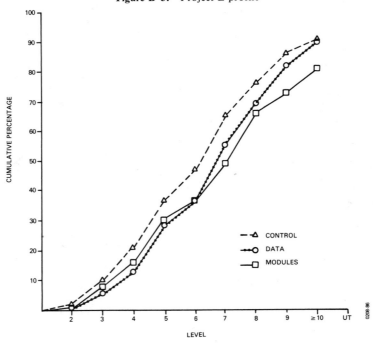

Figure B-6. Project F profile

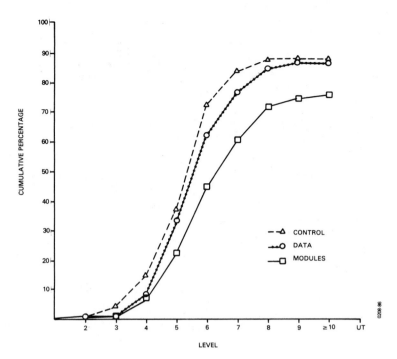

Figure B–7. Project G profile

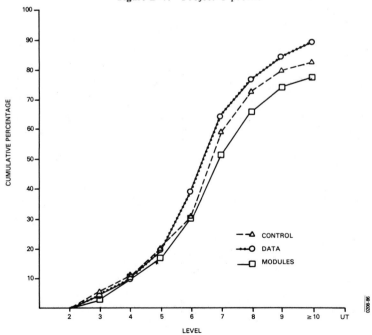

Figure B–8. Project H profile

Appendix C

Software Cost Estimation Parameters

This appendix identifies some basic parameters for software cost estimation that can be extracted from an organization's historical data. Table C–1 shows values based on SEL data used for estimating spacecraft flight dynamics projects [79]. These numbers are provided as examples, not as recommendations for use in other environments.

TABLE C-1. BASIC ESTIMATION PARAMETERS

PHASE	MEASURE		NOMINAL VALUE [c]
REQUIREMENTS ANALYSIS[b]	SIZE:	LINES OF CODE PER SUBSYSTEM	7500
	COST:	HOURS PER SUBSYSTEM	1850
	SCHEDULE:	WEEKS PER SUBSYSTEM PER PERSON	45
PRELIMINARY DESIGN [b]	SIZE:	LINES OF CODE PER MODULE	125
	COST:	HOURS PER MODULE	30
	SCHEDULE:	WEEKS PER MODULE PER PERSON	0.75
DETAILED DESIGN [b]	SIZE:	RELATIVE WEIGHT OF REUSED[d] CODE	0.2
	COST:	HOURS PER DEVELOPED LINE OF CODE	0.3
	SCHEDULE:	WEEKS PER DEVELOPED MODULES PER PERSON	1.0
IMPLEMENTATION	SIZE:	PERCENT GROWTH DURING TESTING	10
	COST:	TESTING PERCENT OF TOTAL EFFORT	25
	SCHEDULE:	TESTING PERCENT OF TOTAL SCHEDULE	30
SYSTEM TESTING	COST:	ACCEPTANCE TESTING PERCENT OF TOTAL EFFORT	5
	SCHEDULE:	ACCEPTANCE TESTING PERCENT OF TOTAL SCHEDULE	10

[a] AT END OF EACH PHASE, BASED ON SEL DATA.
[b] ESTIMATES OF TOTALS, NOT REQUIRED TO COMPLETE.
[c] BASED ON DATA COLLECTED IN THE FLIGHT DYNAMICS ENVIRONMENT.
[d] DOES NOT INCLUDE EXTENSIVELY MODIFIED REUSED MODULE.

S8/9/10

Appendix D

Measurement and Statistical Concepts

This appendix discusses some of the technical issues involved in defining and analyzing software measures. Developing an effective practical measure of some attribute of a software object involves considerations of measurement scale, data collection methods, data validation, and analysis techniques. These issues have concerned software measurement specialists for a long time, as indicated in Chap. 1.

Measurement is a basic tool of engineering, and statistical analysis is a basic tool of the experimental sciences; but collecting and analyzing measures do not make software development an engineering or scientific discipline. Application of established measures, not analysis of potentially useful measurement approaches, characterizes engineering.

Figure D-1 illustrates the evolution of measures from theory to practice. Measurement begins with the formulation of a theory or model. Next, measures quantifying key elements of the theory must be defined and collected. Analysis of the collected data supports the evaluation of the accuracy of the original theory as well as of the effectiveness of the measures themselves. Changes to the theory initiate another round of quantification and evaluation. Once a firm empirical foundation for a theory or model has been established, practical application of the correspond-

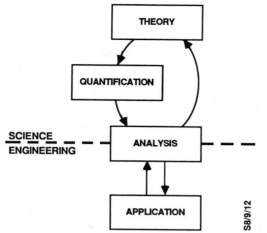

Figure D-1. The evolution of measures

ing measures can begin. Real-world experience often suggests further improvements to the theory and measures.

Because of the intense pressure in the computer industry to reduce the time between innovation and application of new technology, "engineering" practitioners often end up trying to choose among competing measurement approaches, none of which has been thoroughly evaluated by "scientist" researchers. Kearney et al. [2] observed that many measures seem to appear by spontaneous generation in the quantification step, without benefit of theory, evaluation, or application.

Sections D-1 and D-2 review some general principles of measurement and statistics relevant to the quantification and evaluation steps (see Fig. D-1). They will help the reader to recognize some of the difficult issues faced by researchers in producing the results discussed in Chaps. 3, 4, and 5. Almost any published software measurement study can be criticized on the basis of one or more of the considerations discussed here. (Still, progress on a long trip always begins with a first step.)

D-1 DEFINING AND COLLECTING MEASURES

The theory or model developed as the first step (see Fig. D-1) toward measurement defines the characteristics that need to be quantified. Chapter 1 introduced a high-level model of software design. The model's important characteristics included complexity and modularity. The next step is to define appropriate measures of those characteristics. A measure is a set (or scale) of possible values that correspond to variations in an observable characteristic. The usefulness of any measure depends, in part, on how it is constructed (or defined). Concerns during measurement definition include measurement scales, data collection methods, and data validation.

Measurement Scales and Methods

Measurement scales (sets of values) fall into four classes: nominal, ordinal, interval, and ratio. Nominal scales are classifications based on simple characteristics like color or type. Ordinal scales involve a ranking (e.g., from best to worst). Interval scales imply that equal distances between values mean equal differences in characteristic measured. (Time is an example.) Ratio scales have the interval property but also have a definite zero point at which none of the characteristic exists (e.g., length). As shown in Table D-1, the measurement scale affects both data collection and analysis methods (to be discussed later). Sometimes the scale of measurement is uncertain for software development characteristics.

Methods of measurement may be subjective (based on human judgment) or objective (based on physical counts, weight). Only nominal or ordinal levels of measurement can be achieved with subjective methods. Subjective data usually must be collected by means of labor-intensive questionnaires or surveys. Dependence on human judgment means that such measures can be biased and that the exact context of measurement cannot be reproduced. Different observers, or the same observer at different times, often report different ratings. Providing more detailed instructions for performing, the subjective rating improves the consistency and objectivity of the results.

The intellectual nature of the software design process means that important components of it must be measured subjectively. On the other hand, the tangible representation of the design product can be measured objectively for many purposes. Simple tools can automate collection of this type of measure. As the use of design tools like Excelerator® and DesignAid® becomes more widespread, automatic collection and analysis of design measures will become easier.

Another concern is deciding on the right level of detail for measurement. Possible levels of detail include the system, subsystem, module, statement, and operation. The appropriate level of detail for measurement depends on the attribute to

TABLE D-1.   SOME MEASUREMENT CONCERNS

MEASUREMENT SCALE	MEASUREMENT METHODS	ANALYSIS TECHNIQUES
NOMINAL	SUBJECTIVE OBJECTIVE	NONPARAMETRIC EXPLORATORY
ORDINAL	SUBJECTIVE OBJECTIVE	NONPARAMETRIC EXPLORATORY
INTERVAL	OBJECTIVE	PARAMETRIC NONPARAMETRIC EXPLORATORY
RATIO	OBJECTIVE	PARAMETRIC NONPARAMETRIC EXPLORATORY

S8/9/6

be studied. Too gross measures may not be sensitive enough to detect the target attribute. Too detailed measures may be overwhelmed by extraneous factors.

Data Validation, Accuracy, and Extraneous Factors

The measurement practitioner needs to be alert for potential problems in the data. Erroneous data can enter a measurement system at many points. Basic range and spelling checks must be performed. In addition, data can be validated by comparing the data with related data or by collecting the same data in more than one way. Reviewing periodic reports or listings of the data often reveals data problems.

The accuracy of the measuring instrument (e.g., ruler or scale) limits the accuracy of measurement. Even in laboratory physics experiments, repeated measurement of the same quantity yields slightly different results. In the uncontrolled field environment of software development, many other factors incidental to the object of measurement affect the outcome of measurement. Because software measurement data relate to individual performance, participants may try to bias even objective data.

Often it is difficult to isolate the effects of a single technology factor (e.g., tool or method) in an actual project. Many technologies tend to be applied together. On the other hand, the results of small laboratory experiments of isolated technologies cannot be relied upon to scale up to the demands of a production environment. Methods and tools often have synergistic effects. However, without measurement, the software enterprise has no evidence that it is using a new technology properly or that it is improving itself over time.

To some extent, these factors can be minimized by appropriate sampling. Selecting a sample that holds a given factor constant for all observations eliminates that factor outright. More often, analysts assume that these potentially disturbing factors have been randomized enough to be ignored. Unfortunately, strong random effects may mask the relationship the analyst is attempting to understand. Often sample sizes in software engineering studies are small, so it is difficult to show statistical significance in the presence of strong random effects.

Given all the uncertainty inherent in the early stages of measurement, it is not surprising that many practitioners throw down their pencils in frustration. Nevertheless, as DeMarco [11] exhorts: Poor measures are better than none; and crude data are better than guessing unaided. This book demonstrates that a systematic measurement approach leads eventually to sophisticated and useful measures.

D-2   PARAMETRIC, NONPARAMETRIC, AND COMMON-SENSE STATISTICS

Evaluation is the next step in measurement after quantification. Usually, it involves some degree of statistical data processing. Evaluation must be related to an underlying model to be meaningful. Statistics does not substitute for theoretical thinking. It is a tool for evaluating hypotheses and models (which still need to be developed). It enables us to draw inferences about the world based on incomplete and noisy data. In this sense, "statistics is a poor man's substitute for contrived laboratory experiments in which all important relevant variables have been controlled" (Blalock [12], p. 6).

The sheer magnitude and complexity of software development projects make controlled experiments on a realistic scale impractical. Thus, software engineering principles can never achieve the confidence of engineering principles based on a laboratory science. That doesn't mean software developers don't need engineering principles, however. Statistics is one tool that helps obtain them.

The ready availability of statistical software packages has contributed to an explosive growth in the number (if not quality) of statistical studies reported [13]. Statistics is fast replacing common sense as the heuristic of choice for problem solving in some areas. Still, the analyst needs to apply common sense in addition to statistics. For example, cause-effect relationships in statistical associations are often misinterpreted. Sometimes none of the associated variables qualifies as a "cause" of the others. Time ordering provides one criterion for distinguishing cause from effect. Generally, a cause precedes an effect.

A real understanding of software measurement requires a basic understanding of statistics. The following discussion is intended as an aid to memory rather than as a tutorial. Three mutually supportive approaches to statistical analysis exist: parametric statistics, nonparametric statistics, and exploratory data analysis. The specific technique selected depends on the type of measure analyzed, nature of the underlying data distribution, and current state of the analyst's understanding of the problem and the data.

Parametric ("Normal") Statistics

Parametric statistics associate a probability of error with an assertion (hypothesis) or trend (model). In theory, these techniques require interval or ratio level measures that follow a normal distribution (see Fig. D-2). The normal distribution is a very special case: The population mean, median, and mode are all equal to each other; 68 percent of the data falls within one standard deviation (σ) of the population mean (μ). In practice, parametric statistics can be applied to most unimodal symmetric distributions with confidence. Following are some important terms from parametric statistics:

- *Sample*—one or more items drawn from a larger population but assumed to be representative of that population.
- *Mean* ($\bar{x}$)—the arithmetic average of a sample.
- *Median*—the middle observation of a sample (in rank order from highest to lowest).

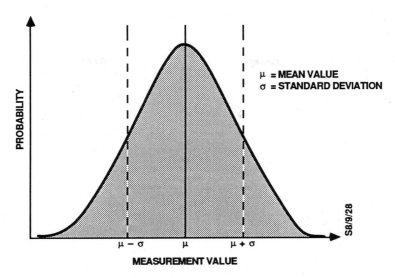

Figure D-2.   The "normal" distribution

- *Mode*—the most common value observed in a sample.
- *Standard deviation* (s)—a measure of the dispersion of values in a sample relative to its mean. A small standard deviation indicates that values cluster closely around the mean.
- *Linear regression*—technique for computing a linear equation relating two or more variables.
- *Correlation coefficient* (r)—a measure of the strength of the linear (or other) regression relationship between two variables. It usually ranges from -1 to $+1$. A correlation coefficient of zero means the variables are independent. A score near $+1$ indicates that values of the variables move together in the same direction (positively correlated). A score near -1 indicates that values of the variables move in opposite directions (negatively correlated).
- *Hypothesis test*—technique for deciding whether or not two parameters are equal to each other, or whether a single parameter is equal to a specified value.
- *Significance* (p)—the probability that an observed relationship (e.g., correlation coefficient, difference in sample means) may be due to chance alone. Most statistics texts recommend use of the 0.05 significance level (5 percent chance of error).*

---

*Unless otherwise specified, in this book the statement that a relationship or difference is significant means that there is less than 5 percent chance that the relationship or difference is due to chance.

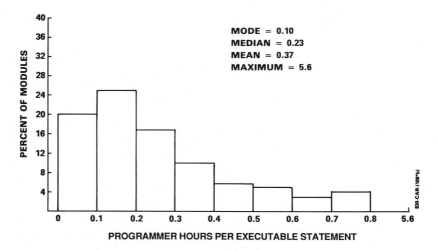

Figure D–3a.   Distribution of development cost

The population mean (μ) and standard deviation (σ) are the parameters of the normal distribution, the basis of the most popular regression and hypothesis-testing techniques. Sample statistics like the mean ($\bar{x}$) and standard deviation (s) approximate the corresponding population parameters (which are often unknown).

Other Statistics

Nonparametric statistics avoid making assumptions about the distribution of the data. These techniques work well with all levels of measurement, including nominal

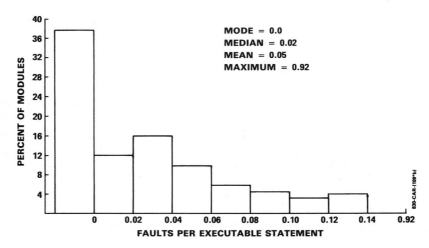

Figure D–3b.   Distribution of fault rate

and ordinal. However, some information will be lost if the data truly do follow a normal distribution with a ratio or interval scale. Relatively infrequent events (like a module demonstrating a fault) usually do not exhibit normal distributions.

Figures D–3a and D–3b provide two examples from the author's data. Because of the nonnormal (compare with Fig. D–2) distributions of cost and fault rate (at the module level) shown in the figures, the author adopted a nonparametric approach to these data (as shown in Chap. 4).

Exploratory data analysis (EDA) is a common-sense, graphics-oriented approach to statistics. Rather than attempting to assign probabilities, EDA focuses on trends. EDA provides the information necessary to choose the appropriate parametric or nonparametric technique for a "definitive" analysis of the data.

Many investigators err by starting to analyze their data with parametric techniques before they have looked at the data in detail. Always begin by examining the data distribution (e.g., Figs. D–3a and D–3b). Romeu and Gloss-Soler [14] suggest that studies of software development should always employ nonparametric techniques because of uncertainty over the level of the measurement scale. Software size, for example, is not deterministic; different implementations of the same function may produce programs of different sizes. Choosing the wrong analysis technique often produces erroneous or misleading results.

References

1. W. E. Perry, "Effective Methods of EDP Quality Assurance," in *Handbook of Software Quality Assurance,* ed. G. G. Schulmeyer and J. I. McManus (New York: Van Nostrand Reinhold, 1987), pp. 408–430.

2. J. K. Kearney, R. L. Sedlmeyer, et al., "Software Complexity Measurement," *Communications of the ACM,* 29, no. 11 (November 1986), 1044–1058.

3. J. C. Browne and M. Shaw, "Toward a Scientific Basis for Software Evaluation," in *Software Metrics: An Analysis and Evaluation,* ed. A. J. Perlis et al. (Cambridge, Mass.: MIT Press, 1981), pp. 19–40.

4. C. V. Ramamoorthy, W. Tsai, T. Yamaura, and A. Bhide, "Metrics Guided Methodology," *Proceedings IEEE Ninth International Conference on Software and Applications,* October 1985, pp. 111–120.

5. J. A. McCall, P. K. Richards, and G. F. Walters, *Factors in Software Quality,* Rome Air Development Center, RADC-TR-369, November 1977.

6. V. R. Basili, "Quantitative Evaluation of Software Methodology," *Proceedings First Pan-Pacific Computer Conference,* September 1985.

7. R. L. Glass, "Standards and Enforcers: Do They Really Help Achieve Software Quality" *Journal of Systems and Software,* 7 (June 1987), 87–88.

8. J. M. Juran, "Basic Concepts," in *Quality Control Handbook,* ed. J. M. Juran et al. (New York: McGraw-Hill, 1974).

9. D. M. Weiss and V. R. Basili, "Evaluating Software Development by Analysis of Changes: Some Data from the Software Engineering Laboratory," *IEEE Transactions on Software Engineering,* 11, no. 2 (February 1985), 157–168.

10. B. W. Boehm, *Software Engineering Economics* (Englewood Cliffs, N.J.: Prentice-Hall, 1981).

11. T. DeMarco, *Controlling Software Projects* (Englewood Cliffs, N.J.: Prentice-Hall, 1982).

12. H. M. Blalock, Jr., *Social Statistics,* 2nd ed. (New York: McGraw-Hill, 1972).

13. R. Hooke, "Getting People to Use Statistics Properly," *American Statistician,* 34, no. 1 (February 1980), 39–42.

14. J. L. Romeu and S. A. Gloss-Soler, "Some Measurement Problems Detected in the Analysis of Software Productivity Data and Their Statistical Consequences," *Proceedings IEEE Seventh International Conference on Software and Applications,* November 1983, pp. 17–24.

15. V. R. Basili and K. Freburger, "Programming Measurement and Estimation in the Software Engineering Laboratory," *Journal of Systems and Software,* 2 (1981), 47–57.

16. D. N. Card, "A Software Technology Evaluation Program," *Information and Software Technology,* 29, no. 6 (August 1987), 291–300.

17. J. D. Valett and F. E. McGarry, "A Summary of Software Measurement Experience in the Software Engineering Laboratory," *Proceedings Twenty-first Hawaii International Conference on Systems Sciences,* January 1988.

18. S. T. Redwine and W. E. Riddle, "Software Technology Maturation," *Proceedings IEEE Eighth International Conference on Software Engineering,* August 1985, pp. 189–200.

19. B. Curtis, "In Search of Software Complexity," *Proceedings IEEE Workshop on Quantitative Software Models,* October 1979, pp. 95–106.

20. M. H. Halstead, *Elements of Software Science* (New York: Elsevier, 1977).

21. J. P. Malenge, Critique de la Physique du Logiciel, trans. M. Marcotty. University of Nice, Pub. Inf. IMAN-P-23, October 1980.

22. N. S. Coulter, "Software Science and Cognitive Psychology," *IEEE Transactions on Software Engineering,* 9, no. 2 (March 1983), 166–171.

23. A. M. Lister, "Software Science—The Emperor's New Clothes?" *Australian Computer Journal,* 14, no. 2 (May 1982), 66–71.

24. P. G. Hamer and G. D. Frewin, "M. H. Halstead's Software Science—A Critical Examination," *Proceedings IEEE Sixth International Conference on Software Engineering,* 1982, pp. 197–206.

25. V. Y. Shen, S. D. Conte, and H. E. Dunsmore, "Software Science Revisited: A Critical Analysis of the Theory and Its Empirical Support," *IEEE Transactions on Software Engineering,* 9, no. 2 (March 1983), 155–165.

26. A. Fitzsimmons and T. Love, "A Review and Evaluation of Software Science," *ACM Computing Surveys,* 10, no. 1 (March 1978), 3–18.

27. D. N. Card and W. W. Agresti, "Resolving the Software Science Anomaly," *Journal of Systems and Software,* 7 (March 1987), 29–35.

28. V. R. Basili, "Evaluating Software Development Characteristics: Assessment of Software Measures in the Software Engineering Laboratory," *Proceedings Sixth Annual Software Engineering Workshop,* Goddard Space Flight Center, SEL-81-013, December 1981.

29. A. J. Albrecht and J. E. Gaffney, "Software Function, Source Lines of Code, and Development Effort Prediction: A Software Science Validation," *IEEE Transactions on Software Engineering,* 9, no. 6 (November 1983), 639–648.

30. T. J. McCabe, "A Complexity Measure," *IEEE Transactions on Software Engineering,* 2, no. 4 (December 1976), 308–320.

31. T. Gilb, *Software Metrics* (Cambridge, Mass.: Winthrop, 1977).

32. G. J. Myers, "An Extension to the Cyclomatic Measure of Program Complexity," *ACM SIGPLAN Notices,* October 1977.

33. M. Evangelist, "Software Complexity Metric Sensitivity to Program Structuring Rules and Other Issues in Software Complexity," paper presented at Sixth Minnowbrook Workshop on Software Performance Evaluation, July 1983.

34. W. Hansen, "Measurement of Program Complexity by the Pair (Cyclomatic Number, Operator Count)," *ACM SIGPLAN Notices,* March 1978.

35. C. L. McClure, "A Model for Program Complexity Analysis," *Proceedings IEEE Third International Conference on Software Engineering,* May 1978, pp. 149–157.

36. L. A. Belady and C. J. Evangelisti, "System Partitioning and Its Measure," *Journal of Systems and Software,* 2 (1981), 23–39.

37. S. M. Henry and D. G. Kafura, "Software Structure Metrics Based on Information Flow," *IEEE Transactions on Software Engineering,* 7, no. 5 (September 1981), 510–518.

38. S. S. Yau and J. S. Collofello, "Some Stability Measures for Software Maintenance," *IEEE Transactions on Software Engineering,* 6, no. 6 (November 1980), 545–552.

39. J. L. Elshoff, "Analysis of Some Commercial PL/I Programs," *IEEE Transactions on Software Engineering,* 2, no. 2 (June 1976), 113–120.

40. S. Woodfield, "Enhanced Effort Estimation by Extending Basic Programming Models to Include Modularity Factors" (Ph.D. dissertation, Purdue University, 1980).

41. M. R. Woodward, M. A. Hennell, and D. Hedley, "A Measure of Control Flow Complexity in Program Text," *IEEE Transactions on Software Engineering,* 5, no. 1 (January 1979), 45–51.

42. W. P. Stevens, G. J. Myers, and L. L. Constantine, "Structured Design," *IBM Systems Journal,* 2 (1972), 115–139.

43. D. L. Parnas, "On the Criteria to Be Used in Decomposing Systems into Modules," *Communications of the ACM,* 15, no. 12 (December 1972), 1053–1058.

44. G. J. Myers, *Reliable Software Through Composite Design* (Princeton, N.J.: Petrocelli/Charter, 1975).

45. D. N. Card, V. E. Church, and W. W. Agresti, "An Empirical Study of Software Design Practices," *IEEE Transactions on Software Engineering,* 12, no. 2 (February 1986), 264–271.

46. M. Takahashi and Y. Kamayachi, "An Empirical Study of a Model for Program Error Prediction," *Proceedings IEEE Eighth International Conference on Software Engineering,* August 1985, pp. 330–336.

47. J. B. Lohse and S. H. Zweben, "Experimental Evaluation of Software Design Principles: An Investigation into the Effect of Module Coupling on System Modifiability," *Journal of Systems and Software,* 4 (1984), 301–308.

48. D. A. Troy and S. H. Zweben, "Measuring the Quality of Structured Designs," *Journal of Systems and Software,* 2 (1981), 113–120.

49. D. N. Card, G. T. Page, and F. E. McGarry, "Criteria for Software Modularization," *Proceedings IEEE Eighth International Conference on Software Engineering,* August 1985, pp. 372–377.

50. R. N. Mathur, "Methodology for Business System Development," *IEEE Transactions on Software Engineering,* 13, no. 5 (May 1987), 593–601.

51. G. Booch, "Object Oriented Design," *IEEE Transactions on Software Engineering,* 12, no. 2 (February 1986), 211–221.

52. G. Benyon-Tinker, "Complexity Measures in an Evolving Large System," *IEEE Workshop on Quantitative Software Models,* October 1979, pp. 117–126.

53. D. H. Hutchens and V. R. Basili, "System Structure Analysis: Clustering with Data Bindings," *IEEE Transactions on Software Engineering,* 11, no. 8 (August 1985), 749–757.

54. J. D. Warnier, *Logical Construction of Programs,* 3rd ed., trans. B. Flanagan. (New York: Van Nostrand Reinhold, 1976).

55. V. R. Basili, R. W. Selby, and T. Phillips, "Metric Analysis and Data Validation across Fortran Projects," *IEEE Transactions on Software Engineering,* 9, no. 7 (1983), 652–663.

56. D. Potier, J. L. Albin, R. Ferreol, and A. Bilodeau, "Experiments with Computer Software Complexity and Reliability," *Proceedings IEEE Sixth International Conference on Software Engineering,* September 1982, pp. 94–101.

57. J. E. Gaffney, "Program Control Complexity and Productivity," *IEEE Workshop on Quantitative Software Models,* October 1979, pp. 140–142.

58. F. E. McGarry, J. D. Valett, and D. L. Hall, "Measuring the Impact of Computer Resource Quality on the Software Development Process and Product," *Proceedings Nineteenth Hawaiian International Conference on System Sciences,* January 1985.

59. G. A. Miller, "The Magical Number Seven, Plus or Minus Two: Some Limits on Our Capacity for Processing Information," *Psychology Review,* 3 (1956), 81–97.

60. S. Rotenstreich and W. E. Howden, "Two-Dimensional Program Design," *IEEE Transactions on Software Engineering,* 12, no. 3 (March 1976), 377–384.

61. D. G. Kafura and S. M. Henry, "Software Quality Metrics Based on Interconnectivity," *Journal of Systems and Software,* 3 (1982), 121–131.

62. D. N. Card, F. E. McGarry, and G. T. Page, "Evaluating Software Engineering Technologies," *IEEE Transactions on Software Engineering,* 13, no. 7 (July 1987), 845–851.

63. J. M. Verner and G. Tate, "A Model for Software Sizing," *Journal of Systems and Software,* 7 (1987), 173–177.

64. A. J. Albrecht, "Measuring Application Development Productivity," *Proceedings IBM Guide/Share Application Development Symposium,* October 1979, pp. 83–92.

65. G. G. Schulmeyer and J. I. McManus, eds., *Handbook of Software Quality Assurance* (New York: Van Nostrand Reinhold, 1987).

66. S. Steppel, T. L. Clark, et al., *Digital System Development Methodology* (Falls Church, VA: Computer Sciences Corporation, 1984).

67. M. E. Fagan, "Design and Code Inspections to Reduce Errors in Program Development," *IBM Systems Journal,* 15, no. 3 (1976), 182–211.

68. M. E. Fagan, "Advances in Software Inspections," *IEEE Transactions on Software Engineering* (July 1986), 744–751.

69. J. H. Dobbins, "Inspections as an Up-Front Quality Technique," in *Handbook of Software Quality Assurance,* ed. G. G. Schulmeyer and J. I. McManus (New York: Van Nostrand Reinhold, 1987), pp. 137–177.

70. T. Pyzdek, *An SPC Primer* (Tucson, AZ: Quality America, 1978).

71. R. H. Dunn, "The Quest for Software Reliability," in *Handbook of Software Quality Assurance,* ed. G. G. Schulmeyer and J. I. McManus (New York: Van Nostrand Reinhold, 1987), pp. 342–384.

72. G. J. Myers, "Test-Case Design," in *The Art of Software Testing* (New York: John Wiley, 1979).

73. P. A. Currit, M. Dyer, and H. D. Mills, "Certifying the Reliability of Software," *IEEE Transactions on Software Engineering,* 12, no. 1 (January 1986), 3–11.

74. F. G. Sayward, "Design of Software Experiments," in *Software Metrics: An Analysis and Evaluation,* ed. A. J. Perlis et al. (Cambridge, Mass.: MIT Press, 1981), pp. 43–57.

75. D. N. Card, R. A. Berg, and T. L. Clark, "Improving Software Quality and Productivity," *Information and Software Technology,* 29, no. 5 (June 1987), 235–241.

76. W. W. Agresti, *New Paradigms for Software Development* (New York, NY: Computer Society Press, 1986).

77. R. Balzer, T. E. Cheatham, and C. Green, "Software Technology in the 1990's: Using a New Paradigm," *IEEE Computer,* 16, no. 11 (November 1983), 39–45.

78. M. Shaw, "Beyond Programming-in-the-Large: The Next Challenges for Software Engineering," *Annual Technical Review* (Pittsburgh, PA: Software Engineering Institute, 1985), pp. 5–14.

79. F. E. McGarry, G. T. Page, and D. N. Card, *An Approach to Software Cost Estimation,* Goddard Space Flight Center, SEL-83-001, February 1984.

80. P. Heidenreich, "Designing for Manufacturability," *Quality Progress* (May 1988), 41–44.

81. W. C. Turner, T. H. Mize, and K. E. Case, *Introduction to Industrial and Systems Engineering* (Englewood Cliffs, N.J.: Prentice-Hall, 1978).

82. V. R. Basili, R. W. Selby, and D. H. Hutchens, "Experimentation in Software Engineering," *IEEE Transactions on Software Engineering* (July 1986), 733–743.

83. R. M. Fortuna, "Beyond Quality: Taking SPC Upstream," *Quality Progress* (June 1988).

84. D. N. Card, D. J. Cotnoir, and C. E. Goorevich, "Managing Software Maintenance Cost and Quality," *Proceedings IEEE Second Conference on Software Maintenance,* July 1987.

Index